The Maverick Mediator

by

Anthony Munday

Published by New Generation Publishing in 2023

Copyright © Anthony Munday 2023

First Edition

The author asserts the moral right under the Copyright, Designs and Patents Act 1988 to be identified as the author of this work.

All Rights reserved. No part of this publication may be reproduced, stored in a retrieval system or transmitted, in any form or by any means without the prior consent of the author, nor be otherwise circulated in any form of binding or cover other than that which it is published and without a similar condition being imposed on the subsequent purchaser.

ISBN
        Paperback   978-1-80369-847-2
        Hardback   978-1-80369-848-9
        eBook   978-1-80369-849-6

www.newgeneration-publishing.com

Preface

Over my decades spent within the executive ranks of numerous industries, rarely have I encountered a professional as motivated, compassionate, and maverick thinking as Anthony. And now, we can all enjoy his insightful leadership insights and authentic storytelling captured over many years of 'in the trenches' real-life experience between the covers of this book; perhaps best described as a user manual for anyone wishing to learn how to cut through the nonsense by applying fundamental, common-sense business thinking to get things done. If you're ready to make a real difference with unconventional wisdom in your toolbox, this is the book for you.

Dennis J. Pitocco
Founder & Chief ReImaginator, 360°
Nation Publisher & Editor-in-Chief,
BizCatalyst 360°

Introduction for The Maverick Mediator

by

Len Bernat, Captain, USMC ret.

Author of *Leadership Matters: Advice from a Career USMC Officer*

I was introduced to Tony by Dennis Pitocco, the founder and CEO of the website Bizcatalyst 360. Dennis made the introduction through the LinkedIn website. Tony was interested in writing a book about the leadership lessons he had learned from his many years on the police force in Great Britain and he was looking for a mentor to guide him through the process. Since I had just released my book, *Leadership Matters: Advice from a Career USMC Officer*, I knew I could guide him through the process of outlining the book, editing the chapters as they were completed, and selecting a publisher for his work. His first book, *The Essential Heart of a Leader* was the result of his dedication to sharing his vast experience with others who desired to expand their leadership skills so that success would be the result.

Tony and I stayed in touch after the publication of his book since we formed a wonderful friendship through the process of getting his first book to the market. I was pleased to see that Tony had become a certified mediator because his experiences with conflict resolution as he discussed in this first book made him a natural for this type of position. So, when he reached out to me to see if I would be willing to help him with his next book, *The Maverick Mediator*, I was more than willing to be a part of this project.

I know that some would wonder why I was willing to help someone whom I had never met face to face, but Tony and I were joined by one very special principle – leadership. Leadership is about taking care of your people by doing the right thing every time – even if doing the right thing puts you at odds with your superiors. Leadership is about people. If you do it right, then your impact on the future of those whom you lead will be immeasurable.

That is what makes his new book, *The Maverick Mediator*, so special. The foundation upon which this book builds is the leadership lessons Tony gained through his years as a police officer and in the many leadership positions he achieved during his career. In the years that he dedicated to the people he served, he witnessed the best of human nature, the worst of human behavior, the failure of those who were in leadership positions but had no leadership qualities, and the conflicts that will arise as egos and self-serving decisions hurt the people for whom the leaders were responsible.

So, building upon the strong leadership principles he gained through years of leading his people in the police force and using lessons learned from resolving conflicts among his people, Tony developed a style for mediation that helps all the parties involved to work together to create a workable solution. From the pre-mediation meeting where he establishes a sense of trust between the parties and himself, to the final resolution meeting where a written agreement that is authored by the participants is prepared, Tony shares with his readers the skills and considerations that must be a part of the process to turn a hostile working environment into a team geared for success. He punctuates his discussion of the process with real-life examples of how these steps, when properly applied, work so effectively. So, if you are currently a certified mediator looking to improve your skillset and success rate or an employer trying to learn more about mediation and how it can resolve some of your internal problems, this is the book you need to read. Let *The Maverick Mediator* be your guide to understanding this important tool for creating a productive team that works in harmony to create success.

Acknowledgments

I would like to thank the following people for their help and support:
Mum and Dad, for everything!
Dennis Pitocco for his steadfast support
Len Bernat for his mentorship and example
Paul for making me a proud Dad.
ACAS and The Centre for Creative Leadership for kind permission to use their materials.

Most of all, the people that I have met over the years who enabled me to learn more about myself, in ways that I could never have done on my own.

About the Author

I had a happy and fulfilling childhood. My family would be described as 'working class', yet neither of my parents ever accepted being placed in a box. For them, the box did not exist.

They considered it criminal not to maximise your talents and to be the best version of yourself that you could be. But at the same time, they were open-minded and gregarious.

From my dad, I inherited an undying devotion to Chelsea Football Club, as those who know me will testify! From my mum, I inherited a voracious appetite for knowledge. I was taught how to read and write when I was four years old before I had begun infant school.

They never accepted the status quo as sacrosanct. They would always strive to understand why things were as they were, and question how things could be done better.

I was taught never to allow myself to be bullied but to push back or, in extremis, fight back. If I was to go down, I'd go down fighting.

We had goals as a family. For example, my dad gave up smoking his beloved pipe in order to save up enough money to buy our first car.

Mum managed the 'car account'. It was one of the few quantity-based targets we had as a family. That was a life lesson for me on the limitations of 'target culture'.

They saved for family holidays and other significant events. Perhaps the most impactful life lesson I learned came from my Mum before starting at the town's only grammar school. The attendees at the single-sex school were, in the main sons of professional people like doctors, lawyers, and accountants. They would be described as 'middle class'.

Mum said, **'People may be richer than you, but no one is better than you.'**

I never forgot that lesson.

The positives of the school were that the pupils' wealth did not confer respect amongst us. It was intellect and intelligence that gained praise and honour. These were assets that were highly prized.

The darker meritocracy was devoted to physical prowess, either on the sports field or by brute force.

The school bully was christened Frederick but was known as 'Fred'. He held sway over most people by sheer terror for his methods of enforcement to obtain money or get people to do his homework. He had a crew of followers who did his bidding.

All was well for me until our paths crossed. Fred decided one lunchtime that a 'conversation' with me was required. I had a clear decision to make. Capitulate or challenge him.

Fred moved into position to deliver pain to me. I became aware that a crowd of pupils had gathered; they formed a semi-circle.

Sounds disappeared.

My head was clear. It was obvious what was about to come my way. He tensed and smiled at me.

I remembered something else Mum used to say to me: 'Get your retaliation in first.' She was very clear that I was not playing by Queensbury Rules when my safety was threatened.

I looked into Fred's eyes and hit his chin with the maximum power of punch that I could muster. He staggered back and I kept up a barrage with my fists until he collapsed to the ground. He had not landed a blow on me. He was enraged and snarling like a wounded bull. He swore at me and tried to get up.

I do not know where this primal rage came from within me, but it was visceral. It was almost like an out-of-body experience. Everything appeared to be in slow motion. I did not recognise myself. I was very calm and dispassionate.

I said to him, 'Have you had enough?'

As he got to his feet, he swung at me. I knew that I had to finish this to ensure that he would never bother me again. So, I punched him as hard as I could on the nose. Blood spattered my right fist.

He was mouthing obscenities at me as he went down again.

'Enough!' he shouted and raised his hands, palms outwards.

I then became aware of someone raising my right arm and saying, 'Munday, King of the Fourth (Form).' There was cheering.

Suddenly, I was aware of an adult hand taking hold of my right arm. It was Mr Clarke, the teacher on duty during the break.

'What is the meaning of this?' he shouted. I was then taken to the headmaster's office.

My subsequent Headmaster's Detention on the following Saturday morning concluded proceedings. But Fred left me alone thereafter, although I did not like the persona I had adopted during the fight.

I was embarrassed. I resolved never to experience such feelings again. And I am pleased to say that I have kept that promise to myself.

On reflection, it would have been a good policy if the 'management' of the school – Headmaster, Deputy Headmaster, and senior teachers – had invested in a system of conflict resolution. A process of mediation might have proven beneficial to Fred, his victims, and the school. The importance of an independent mediator who was both trusted and had the confidence of the school can well be imagined. Instead, a toxic culture of bullying and harassment was tolerated until Fred was subsequently expelled in the Fifth Form.

During my police career, there was very little meaningful professional development that enhanced our emotional intelligence. Learning was of the 'this is what we do here' kind. It was up to the individual officer as to which values, they subscribed to, and which role models they followed.

For example, when dealing with 'sudden deaths', there was often a macabre way we were taught to 'toughen up' so that we could deal with horrific scenarios in a professional manner, without wilting.

An illustration of this was how we were prepared for our first post-mortem. This was to be held at the mortuary of the local hospital.

A group of six probationers (we were not confirmed as officers until after two years of continuous assessment; our services could be dispensed with very easily up to that point) or 'sprogs' were instructed to eat a hearty full English breakfast before visiting the mortuary.

The weather had turned nasty. The sky went dark, and thunder and lightning followed. It was like a scene from a Hammer Horror film!

We nervously filed in and waited for the post-mortem to begin. It was evident that the mortician enjoyed his work. He was chatting with us all the time, inviting us to examine his handiwork. The sound of him breaking a ribcage to access the heart remains with me to this day.

The sounds and smells clung to my uniform throughout that day.

The post-mortem viewing was an example of the 'tough love' that we were subject to. Some of my colleagues had vomited during the procedure; others professed nonchalance. I did neither. I did, however, always remember that a corpse had been a person who was loved and respected by others.

We all dealt with sudden deaths in our own way. Some treated it as a necessary task, chomping on the food they had with them as they filled out the form (Form 12A as I recall).

My perspective was rather different. I tried to empathise with the bereaved in a professional but respectful manner.

I will illustrate this by setting the scene.

Monday, Christmas Eve. Snow was falling that evening when the call came at 8.30pm. The deceased was identified as 'Mrs. X'.

When I arrived at the large Tudor-style, detached property, I rang the bell and a man answered, who confirmed that he was the owner and the deceased was, in fact, his mother who was inside. After inviting us in, we entered a large lounge where there was a large Christmas tree, which was decorated in a Victorian style and the fairy lights were twinkling. There was a large dining table with twelve place settings; the plates hadn't been cleared up and all the adults and children were crying.

I apologised for the intrusion at this time and then turned to look at the TV, which was on ITV and playing *Coronation Street*. It was then that the deceased caught my eye. She was sitting on an armchair in front of a roaring log fire.

I asked, 'Was Mrs. X a fan of *Coronation Street*?'

Several family members agreed that she was. Her son said, 'It was her favourite programme.'

I said, 'Has Mrs. X just finished watching the Christmas special episode?'

Her son said, 'She had her dessert whilst watching it.'

I said, 'If I might say, any unexpected death is a tragedy for many people. Sometimes the deceased can pass all alone, without their nearest and dearest being aware of what has happened, and sometimes for a considerable time.

'Tonight, Mrs. X, your Mum, and Grandma, has clearly enjoyed a wonderful Christmas Eve in the company of her loved ones. You had all enjoyed her company at dinner, and then she watched her favourite programme in front of the fire.

'There is never a good time for anyone of us to pass, but your Mum was at her happiest. If there can be a perfect time for anyone of us to pass, this was such a time.'

The bereaved family thanked me for my empathy and compassion. They said my observations had helped them that evening and would help them going forward.

Policing intervenes with people mostly at the worst of times for them. We have the potential to create trust and confidence in our decision-making or to destroy it henceforth.

Empathy and humanity are traits that serve us well in all communications and dealings with each other, whether as police officers, conflict resolution experts, or workplace mediators.

I can remember when I first became aware of the importance of Emotional Intelligence, or Emotional Quotient (EQ).

It would be unfair for me to describe myself as arrogant; rather, I was oblivious to the impact upon others of my words and behaviours. Matters came to a head for me when, as an experienced sergeant, I made my first application for promotion to inspector.

My line manager called me into his office. He said, 'I could just forward this with a neutral comment to the borough commander. But if I did that, I would be failing in my duty of responsibility to you. You seem oblivious to how much you p**s people off. You would be torn to shreds at the next stage. Therefore, I suggest you withdraw the application. Secondly, think of three senior officers that you do not get on with and ask to see them for feedback on your personal style and why it irks them.'

'Would they do so?' I asked.

'There's only one way to find out,' he replied.

I was fearful and hesitant but did as he suggested.

When I explained the purpose of the proposed meeting, all three readily agreed to meet with me. I asked them to be as candid as possible. It was a struggle for me, but I did not interrupt or be defensive at all. It was eye-opening for me. These people whom I had believed disliked me personally, disabused me of that notion.

They praised my courage in coming to see them and seeking feedback. They each described situations to me which had caused them concern as to my suitability for development and promotion. I learned so much about the downsides in professional terms, of my individuality.

In many respects, they subsequently became my allies. They supported my development. They became critical friends. An invaluable source of data for me about myself.

I never forgot the importance of these lessons.

The other significant milestone of my journey in leadership development was my persistent request to undertake an executive diploma in leadership and management. The learning and qualification were intended by my police organisation to be solely for newly promoted inspectors. I contended that previously there had been no such professional development opportunity for us as now experienced inspectors. It was unfair. The course would be voluntary for us.

I describe aspects of this in my first book *The Essential Heart of a Leader*.

The module 'Coaching as a Leadership Style 'was transformational for me to participate in as it was completely contrary to the still prevalent policing culture of 'command and control'.

Frankly, I was regarded as a maverick in the police force because I put these principles into practice. I was not aware of any other senior leaders in my police organisation who were exponents of this style.

The associated behaviours of micromanagement and strategy by targeting where what gets measured gets done were and are anathema to me.

I understood that the role is not the person. I never talked about those I commanded; rather I spoke about the people I was responsible for. I recognised and understood that the circumstances in which I needed to adopt a more prescriptive style were few and far between. Such situations included murder and rape.

I say, 'Leadership is knowing ourselves and those we are as responsible for as people and behaving accordingly.'

I will share one such example:

I was the duty officer (the senior officer with operational primacy) for my policing Area, which consisted of the Boroughs of Dacorum and Watford /Three Rivers.

It was a beautifully warm and sunny day. Almost idyllic.

We were resolving an armed siege around five o'clock one Wednesday evening when a man dressed in shorts and a tee shirt, and walking a small sausage dog, approached us.

'Who's in charge?' he asked.

'That would be me,' I replied.

What he then said was quite unexpected.

'I've just found the dead body of a girl nearby.'

I heard what he had said but I asked him to repeat it.

This time I studied his nonverbal communication, including body language and tone of voice more intently. He was clearly telling the truth.

This repetition also gave me an invaluable few seconds to clarify my thinking and decision-making. The firearms incident had successfully concluded, and a firearms specialist sergeant was coordinating matters.

I was conscious of the need to be at my most calm and measured in communication, both for my team, and the witness. After all, it is not unusual for a principal witness in a murder to be the offender. Sadly, the victim was nearby. Officers were deployed to protect the scene and the surrounding area. The offender (not the witness) was subsequently arrested, charged, and convicted.

Around nine o'clock that evening I became aware that it was turning dark. I had been running on adrenaline and dealing with a myriad of responsibilities. I recalled that none of us had had a meal break and that the handover of vehicles and briefings by officers to night turn officers, who commenced duty at 10 pm, needed to be organised.

The logistics were dealt with. I knew that there was a large McDonald's in Watford. I phoned the outlet and spoke with the manager. I explained the situation and asked if they could supply sufficient meals for all of us. I told him that I did not know the relevant procurement process but that I would pay on my debit card for our meals. He refused to accept payment in such circumstances.

One of my sergeants was recording my policy decisions. I requested another of my sergeants to visit every officer on this operation and to obtain their individual orders for the food. Initially, he protested and argued that it would be sufficient to order many meals and just distribute them ad hoc.

I explained that this was unsatisfactory because it was my way of saying thank you for your service to all the officers. I was determined that this would happen.

The plan was for a record to be made of the individual orders. Mine would be last on the list. This ensured that my instructions were adhered to. The individual orders were honoured.

Several years after this incident, whenever I meet someone who was involved in that operation, they thank me for thinking of their welfare; and for treating them as individuals in such challenging circumstances.

I have never lost sight of the fact that we are all people with individual characters, personalities, and needs.

I am proud to have been regarded as a maverick by the police. I consider this to be a badge of honour.

'People will forget what you said, people will forget what you did, but people will never forget how you made them feel.'

– Maya Angelou

Contents

Preface: Dennis Pittocco i

Introduction for The Maverick Mediator: Len Bernat.. ii

Acknowledgments vi

About the Author.. vii

Chapter One: The Maverick Mediator. Who is the book designed for? 1

Chapter Two: Why I wrote this book.............4

Chapter Three: Affinity with my First Book: *The Essential Heart of a Leader* 6

Chapter Four: How does Workplace Mediation differ from other forms of Conflict Resolution? 14

Chapter Five: Respectful Mediation 30

Chapter Six: My Epiphany 45

Chapter Seven: The Chrysalis Method. Stage One. Pre-Mediation Meeting or 'Icebreaker' 51

Chapter Eight: The Chrysalis Method of Conflict Resolution: Stage Two - The Individual meeting..66

Chapter Nine: The Chrysalis Method of Conflict Resolution. Stage Three – The Joint Meeting 77

Chapter Ten: The Chrysalis Method of Conflict Resolution. Stage Four – The Review Meeting 91

Chapter Eleven: The Chrysalis Method of Conflict Resolution. Stage Five – Structured Debriefing 102

Chapter Twelve: Coda 115

Chapter One

The Maverick Mediator
Who is the book designed for?

- Workplace Mediators who intend to develop authentic rapport with the participants.
- Workplace Mediators who intend that the participants will develop the necessary trust and confidence in their independence, fairness, neutrality, and impartiality.
- Workplace Mediators who recognise the challenges faced by meeting participants for the first time at the individual meeting.
- Workplace Mediators who believe that the interests of participants are paramount in the mediation process.
- HR professionals who are keen to hone their expertise and understanding of workplace mediation.
- HR professionals who perceive that invoking grievance procedures and misconduct proceedings deals with the symptoms rather than the cause of workplace conflict.

- HR professionals who recognise that their position within organisations, or as 'outsourced support' is perceived as being part of 'management' by potential participants in workplace mediation.
- Managers and Supervisors who wish to understand the principles of authentic workplace mediation and how that knowledge will benefit themselves and their organisation.
- Managers and Supervisors who would like to understand how and why invoking grievance procedures and misconduct Proceedings may fail to deal with the core issues in workplace conflict, which may exacerbate the negative impact on the business, compared with mediation.
- Employment Law Solicitors and Barristers who are seeking an effective way to shift themselves from their ingrained litigious mindset because of their professional development.
- Chief Executive Officers who intend to become better informed about how workplace mediation can benefit their people and organisations.
- Students undertaking Business Studies who intend to learn more about

workplace mediation and how it can benefit them in their future business life.

Chapter Two

Why I wrote this book.

This is not intended to be a manual on how to be a workplace mediator. There are excellent training courses and continuing professional development (CPD) run by the Advisory, Conciliation, and Arbitration Service (ACAS) for internal workplace mediators. The training courses are accredited. UK Mediation Limited offers the only Level 4 qualification in Mediation that is accredited by AIM, Ofqual, and UK Mediation. The Civil Mediation Council also offers training in various forms of mediation, including workplace mediation.

It is the mindset that I adopt that truly places the interests of the participants at the heart of the process.

In my opinion, some forms of mediation are more akin to bartering or negotiation; the mediator seeks common ground between the position of the parties. I do not refer to 'parties' in workplace mediation, but to 'participants', it is a more inclusive, less adversarial term.

I wrote this book to demystify the term 'mediation'. The book deals exclusively with my perspective on workplace mediation. The title 'The Maverick Mediator' was chosen because, in my professional life, I have often been regarded as a maverick. The Oxford English Dictionary defines 'maverick' as an unorthodox or independent-minded person. I do not seek to be contrary for the sake of it. However, if I consider a different approach is beneficial for the required outcome, then that is what I develop and adopt. Perhaps the strongest reason for writing this book is for those people who consider workplace mediation a 'soft option'. I trust that by the time you have finished reading my book, you will understand that this is a misconception.

Chapter Three

Affinity with my First Book: *The Essential Heart of a Leader*.

There are several common themes in both of my books:
- My maverick mindset.
- A desire to understand individuals rather than a stereotype.
- A focus on the interests of the person rather than on their position.
- The critical importance of developing trust and confidence in my professional capability.
- The responsibility for effective 'conflict resolution' lies with the supervisor or manager rather than with the Human Resources personnel.
- **Leadership is knowing ourselves and those we are responsible for as people and behaving accordingly.** This is a quote of mine that encapsulates my values and ethics.

I have seen a definition of 'maverick', that defines the term as being an unorthodox or independent-minded person (Oxford English Dictionary).

The Predictive Index describes 'mavericks' thus:

Mavericks are visionaries who want to achieve what's never been achieved before.

They're not fans of the status quo and will shake things up.

Mavericks tend to be innovative, influential, daring, and direct, with a remarkably high tolerance for taking chances.

Characteristics of a Maverick

- Innovative.
- Goal-oriented.
- Visionary.
- Flexible.

Common Drivers

- Opportunities to influence.
- Freedom from rules and controls.
- Variety.
- Competition.

Blind Spots

- Technical work.
- Limited attention to detail.
- Delegates with loose follow-up.

- May appear tough-minded.

This thumbnail sketch describes my character succinctly:

During my police career, I was obliged to follow criminal law, road traffic legislation, other statute law, and the common law. However, I regarded custom and practice, defined by the awful term 'this is what we do here' with an objective, enquiring mindset, and drew my own conclusions.

My principal considerations were: *Why are we doing this? What is the supposed purpose? Does it make sense? How could this be done better for all concerned?*

My overarching principle as a leader was that those people that I was responsible for, NOT those I commanded, were precious people. They were not owned by me but rather leased to me whilst on duty.

It was my responsibility to develop my people to the maximum extent possible so that in their daily duties, they would be ethical and deliver the best service to those that needed our assistance in their hour of need.

Additionally, I had a responsibility to ensure that I delivered them back to their families in the best psychological state possible.

The wide-ranging panoply of police involvement in the lives of people is rarely well-accepted by our 'customers'. The resultant rate of divorce amongst the police – higher than the military – in the United Kingdom bears eloquent testimony to the inordinate levels of stress that build up over time on police officers and, by extension, their families, and friends.

I recognised that the officer or police staff member was performing a role whilst on duty. That is not the same as the person hidden from direct view. The culture of coping makes good camouflage.

Sadly, the statistics of police suicides are truly disturbing.

The Office for National Statistics (ONS) provides the following data.

In 2020/21 there were 191 police-related fatalities in England and Wales, compared with 206 in the previous reporting year of 2019/20. Of these 191 fatalities, 54 were suicides, 25 were road traffic fatalities, 19 were deaths in or following police custody, with one fatal shooting in 2020/21.

These sobering numbers confirm the basic truth that I firmly believe: Leadership is knowing ourselves and those we are

responsible for as people and behaving accordingly.

I was fortunate to be trained in active listening, body language, and non-verbal communication.

Essentially, HEAR what is said, how it is said, what is not said, rather than just LISTEN.

Such expertise I believe is a fundamental aspect of the toolkit for a mediator. It is accepted practice for many fellow mediators to refer to the people directly involved in the process, as 'parties'. I do not subscribe to using this term in this context as it is fundamentally, if not fatally, flawed.

It speaks to me of litigation in court proceedings and is therefore an adversarial term. It reinforces the mindset of such mediators who use it in terms of 'winners' and 'losers'.

Mediation is win-win because there is no hierarchy of importance of needs amongst those taking part in the mediation. There is a shared objective to achieve an inclusive and shared positive outcome.

The potential for other mediators to prejudge people and their situation is therefore considerable. This capacity can be further enhanced by the provision of detailed background by the client organisation on the individuals and the history of conflict between them.

Colleagues in the legal profession are familiar with and expectant of a detailed 'brief 'about the matters in hand in future legal proceedings. They will either specialise in prosecuting offenders or defending victims. Some alternate their role as part of their professional development.

They are first and foremost litigators who are required and expected to win their cases on behalf of their clients.

A learned judge presides over proceedings, which are usually held in public (except for specified reasons like national security).

In jury trials, the jurors determine which of the lawyers has been most convincing.

It must be extremely challenging for legal professionals who are mediators to forget their ingrained mindset and adopt a role that requires neutrality, fairness, objectivity, and impartiality.

I say this because for me, any information beyond the names and email addresses of the participants, for initial contact purposes, risks tainting my required mindset with the subjective perspective of others.

The parallel with my communication with victims, witnesses, suspects, and other officers whilst I was a police officer is real. It was vitally important for me as a police officer (and for a manager or supervisor in an organisation today), to be authentically objective, impartial, neutral, and fair when speaking with members of the team.

The creation of trust and confidence in the professional standards of the manager or mediator is critical in ensuring that the individuals concerned in a situation feel able to speak up and reveal the core issues that concern them.

You can therefore understand why I refer to the people who have agreed to take part in the mediation process as 'participants'. This is a neutral term and speaks to shared involvement and responsibility.

In my book, *The Essential Heart of a Leader*, I recognised that it was my responsibility to lead, manage, and motivate my teams and departments. This was achieved by my knowing them as individual people.

Similarly, this pertains to managers and supervisors today.

An accessible and knowledgeable Human Resources team is a vital support to any organisation. However, they do not have the line-management responsibilities of managers and supervisors beyond their own department or team.

In my professional opinion, the role of Human Resources is to support and empower managers, so that they can manage people effectively and fairly.

I have seen far too many examples of poor managers seeking to absolve themselves of their professional responsibility by requiring HR to activate formal processes rather than the manager having the initial 'difficult conversations' to ascertain what is actually going on.

Managers knowing how to converse and communicate with people are not 'soft skills'; in my view, they are ESSENTIAL SKILLS.

- Managers need to manage.
- Supervisors need to supervise.
- Mediators need to mediate.

In all three contexts, the ability to create an environment where people feel confident to speak from the heart is essential.

Chapter Four

How does workplace mediation differ from other forms of Conflict Resolution?

The following tables are reproduced with the kind permission of ACAS. They were presented by Professor Peter Urwin, University of Westminster, from the ACAS London Conference of February 2022.

ACAS is the Advisory, Conciliation, and Arbitration Service, which is the independent public body that receives money from the UK Government. They work with millions of employers and employees each year to improve workplace relationships.

CONVENTIONAL NEGOTIATION

- Getting the best deal— the largest slice of the pie
- Outcome determined by bargaining power
- Focus on positions

Think about how you would negotiate a starting salary for a new member of staff – what are the key factors?

- *The going rate*
- *Pay of similar workers in the business*
- *How much do they want/need the job*
- *Are there alternative candidates?*

In the organisational world, the dynamics of power can be at play. That is, in general terms, the further up the corporate ladder, the more 'clout' that person has with more junior colleagues.

In the event of the persons being on the same level, then experience, years served or in post, or significance of the department in the 'pecking order' comes into play.

Conflict is inevitable.

- Conflict is an inherent and unavoidable part of the employment relationship.
- In the UK, one-third of workers experience conflict at work every year.
- Most conflicts remain 'hidden'.

BUT
- 4 in 10 workers who experience conflict report reduced motivation.
- 56% report stress, anxiety, and depression.

Workplace Mediation is a win-win for the participants. This is the principal difference from other forms of mediation.

What do I mean by this statement?

In workplace mediation, the participants, facilitated by the mediator, work together to devise, develop, and deliver their desired future of positive and sustainable outcomes.

This is confirmed in written form by the Written Agreement. This is codified and confirmed. It outlines the ways in which the participants will behave toward one another. It is a moral contract.

I will touch upon these other forms of dispute resolution.

Other forms of conflict resolution include:

Arbitration.

- This is where an external person listens to the issues from all sides and then recommends a solution to them. The proposal can be declared binding in advance of discussions and negotiations.
- The extent of 'buy-in' from the people in conflict is often dependent upon matters of power and influence rather than a moral duty.
- The arbitrator will deal with the issues as presented to them. There is not necessarily a 'deep dive' into the core issues. These may remain and can flare up in the future.

Grievance Procedures.

- Organisations invariably have access to the advice—in some form or another—of Human Resources (HR) people.
- This procedure is invoked when employees behave in such a manner towards each other that behaviours breach accepted standards of behaviour (e.g., bullying) and communication between them has broken down.
- The accepted standards are typically defined and explained in the policies of the organisation.
- The nature of the infraction has breached the code of conduct established in the organisation.
- An investigation to prove or disprove the allegation will be set up. The standard of proof is the civil standard on the balance of probabilities.
- There will be a finding that the allegation is either proven or not proven.
- The accused person is entitled to be accompanied to any meeting by a friend or staff association representative for pastoral support.
- There is no drive to repair fractured relationships. The finding of the

investigation will apportion blame and the person's personal record will be endorsed accordingly.
- Thus at least one person 'loses'.
- If the allegation cannot be proven, then the accuser will also be dissatisfied.
- The impact on the culture of the organisation may not always be positive because of invoking the grievance procedure.
- This can be a tactic used by wilfully poor performers to deflect attention from their performance and to seek to 'muzzle' a manager trying to manage.
- Managers can become wary of such a tactic of repeating grievances and either ignore the poor performer, they may change roles, or leave the organisation altogether.
- It is essential that managers receive appropriate support from HR and a senior colleague to ensure that the right lessons have been learned.

Misconduct

- It is important that the most serious breaches of accepted standards are

treated effectively, appropriately, and in a timely fashion.
- The impact of unchecked poor behaviours on people within the organisation and their morale and performance can be considerable.
- Customer service can deteriorate, and the brand reputation can suffer.
- Discipline should be reserved for the most egregious breaches of company standards.
- Managers should always be supported by HR and a senior member of staff.
- The most serious of cases can be held to be gross misconduct. These include criminal behaviours such as discrimination, assault, or theft.
- Sanctions for such offences include instant dismissal or a reduction in the role.
- In this context, it would be appropriate to describe the people involved as 'parties'. One or more of the parties is accused of an offence or offences. The other party is the victim or the victims.
- This can be seen to be a quite different dynamic from that of workplace mediation.

- The participants are in an adversarial situation as opposed to working together towards a common goal.

Employment Tribunals (ET).

- These are the formal legal proceedings, often presided over by a judge, whereby barristers or other persons with a right of audience, argue the case and seek redress for the perceived wrongs done to them.
- All options to avoid the ET should have been tried or at least considered. This includes mediation.
- Clearly by this stage, we can talk of parties.
- One side will win their case.
- Sanctions will be applied.
- Most importantly, it will not cause relationships to be healed. Quite often, it is just the opposite.

Resignation.

- The loss of people from your organisation is an expensive action. Patterns of people leaving should always

be a concern for HR and the Senior Leadership Team (SLT).
- This is where exit interviews are pure gold. They provide the organisation with the opportunity to ascertain causes and to do something about it.
- It is famously said that people do not leave poor organisations; they leave poor managers.

The Costs of Workplace Conflict

Thanks to ACAS for granting their kind permission to use their slides from the ACAS Mediation Conference of February 2022. Professor Peter Urwin, University of Westminster.

estimating-the-costs-of-workplace-conf

The ACAS 2021 Study Estimating the Cost of workplace conflict has some startling statistics.

Executive summary

This report is the first to systematically map the incidence of conflict across UK workplaces, showing how this impacts individuals, and their employers, estimating the overall cost to UK organisations.

Key findings

In 2018–19, just over one-third (35%) of respondents to a Certificate in Human Resources Practice (CIPD) study reported having experienced either:
1) an isolated dispute or incident of conflict (26%) and/or
2) an ongoing difficult relationship (24% – including conflict with parties external to the organisation) over the last 12 months.

Using these findings, we estimate that 9.7 million employees experienced conflict in 2018–19.

The vast majority of employees who experienced conflict stayed with the organisation and just 5% resigned as a result. A slightly higher proportion of respondents reported taking time off as sickness absence (9%). However, 40% reported being less motivated, and more than half (56%) reported stress, anxiety, and/or depression.

We estimate that an average of 485,800 employees resign each year because of conflict. The cost of recruiting replacement employees amounts to £2.6 billion each year, whilst the cost to employers of lost output as new employees get up to speed, amounts to £12.2 billion – an overall estimate of £14.9 billion each year. A further 874,000 employees are estimated to take sickness absences each year because of conflict, at an estimated cost to their organisations of £2.2 billion.

The vast majority of those who suffer from stress, anxiety, and/or depression due to conflict continue to work. This 'presenteeism' has a negative impact on productivity with an annual cost estimated between £590 million and £2.3 billion.

1 in 5 employees take no action in response to the conflict in which they are involved, while around one quarter discuss the issue with the other person involved in the conflict. Just over half of all employees discuss the matter with their manager, HR, or union representative. In total, informal discussions cost UK organisations an estimated £231 million each year.

In 2018–19, 5% of respondents took part in some form of workplace mediation, whether internally or externally provided, at an estimated cost of £140 million. Nearly three-quarters of those who underwent mediation (74%) also reported that their conflict had been fully or largely resolved. While this points to the potential efficacy of the process in terms of resolution, the wider impacts were more mixed, as we discuss in more detail below.

We estimate that there are an average of 374,760 formal grievances each year. The average cost in management time of a formal grievance is estimated at £951, giving a total cost across the economy of £356 million. In addition, there are an estimated 1.7 million formal disciplinary cases in UK organisations each year. The estimated average cost of each disciplinary case is approximately £1,141 – resulting in an economy-wide total cost of £2 billion. Furthermore, our estimates suggest that an average of 428,000 employees are dismissed each year, and replacing them costs UK organisations an estimated £13.1 billion.

We calculate that 136,249 early conciliation (EC) notices were submitted across the UK, including 132,711 submitted to ACAS in 2018–19, indicating an intention to pursue an employment tribunal claim.

The total cost of management time spent dealing with potential and actual litigation is estimated at £282 million each year with a further £264 million spent on legal fees.

In addition, we calculate that £225 million in compensation is awarded against employers per year. The largest proportion of the costs of conflict are connected to an ending of the employment relationship – either through resignation or dismissal. Costs in the early stages of conflict are relatively low – these start to mount if employees continue to work while ill and/or take time off work through sickness absence. The use of formal processes pushes costs higher; however, costs escalate very quickly as soon as employees either resign or are dismissed.

This analysis estimates the overall total annual cost of conflict to employers (including management and resolution) at £28.5 billion.

This represents an average of just over £1,000 for every employee in the UK each year, and just under £3,000 annually for each individual involved in conflict (see endnote 1). It points to a clear link between the well-being of employees and organisational effectiveness.

Implications for Policy and organisational practice

Investment in effective and early conflict resolution designed to build positive employment relationships may have a very significant return.

The average costs of conflict where employees did not engage with their managers, HR, or union representatives, were higher than where such discussions took place. Furthermore, where conflict spiralled into formal procedures, costs were more than three times the costs associated with informal resolution.

Organisations need to place much greater emphasis on repairing employment relationships in the event of conflict and taking action at early points to address issues of capability and poor performance. Moreover, the analysis provides support for approaches to disciplinary issues that focus on learning and avoiding blame. However, to achieve this, managers need to be provided with the core people skills to have quality interactions with their staff.

The results provide strong arguments for a rebalancing of policy – decreasing the emphasis on legal compliance and effectiveness of the tribunal system, towards the resolution of conflict within organisations. These findings are particularly salient given the impacts of the COVID-19 pandemic on employment relationships. They provide clear support for policies that seek to preserve employment where viable in the longer term. It is likely that conflict will be more likely as organisations adapt to a new normal and problems suppressed during the crisis start to rise to the surface, requiring effective organisational responses.

Finally, a more sustained shift to remote working and the potential acceleration of automation will create new challenges for the effective management of people, placing a premium on the skills needed to prevent, manage, and resolve conflict.

The following tables present some of these key findings in a visual form.

THE COSTS OF CONFLICT

In the UK conflict costs more than £4,000 per worker per year
Wasted management time
• Early management interventions are low cost and represent good value for money • As conflict escalates the burden on management increases
Reduced productivity
• Those in conflict report reduced engagement • Spill-over effects in to the team and organization
Absence and presenteeism
• Around 1 in 10 workers in the UK involved in conflict take time off work as a result • The vast majority of workers who suffer mental ill-health due to conflict carry on working but their productivity is between 15 and 30% lower
Turnover
• Costs of replacement, recruitment and training • Replacement workers have lower productivity

The essence of the message is clear. Appropriate early intervention by supervisors and managers can help to mitigate the costs of conflict in the workplace.

Some of these symptoms will be less obvious and visible than others.

Morale, absenteeism, presenteeism, or 'quiet quitting' can be ascertained more readily by those who know their team as people. The direct costs of replacing those who have resigned can be easily ascertained. Less apparent will be the indirect costs associated with recruitment, the time and money required to train the new employee and lower productivity of new workers.

Prevention is always better than cure!

Similarly, as the next table shows, the direct and indirect costs of conflict escalate.

In the event of a conflict arising, you can see why the alternative of workplace mediation is very positive for both the participants and the wider organisation. The value of previously conflicted parties being facilitated to work together to create and design a positive future for themselves is considerable. The benefits of a positive business relationship on morale and productivity are evident.

The spillover into their private lives is of real benefit to previously conflicted, often traumatised people. The enhanced quality of family life benefits everyone.

THE ESCALATING COST OF CONFLICT

Individual raises the issue with manager	£70
Facilitated meeting with manager, HR and union representative	£150
Workplace mediation	£1500
Individual brings a formal grievance	£2550
Employee is absent due to stress, anxiety and depression	
Employee resigns	£30,014
Employee brings employment tribunal claim	

Chapter Five

Respectful Mediation

My overarching principle in workplace mediation is to recognise that the people directly involved in the process are invariably traumatised. My direct experience tells me that workplace relationships that have deteriorated and fractured have taken months, sometimes years, to become intolerable before client organisations contact me to discuss their situation.

The importance of recognising that the bullying, 'gaslighting', and how ineffective the grievance procedure was in resolving matters, had an impact on me that I have never forgotten.

In my case, early intervention by a manager on my behalf (including workplace mediation), would have saved me, my loved ones, and the organisation so much awful stress. I trust that my telling you my story will help to explain why I am such a passionate advocate of 'independent workplace mediation'.

I know how awful stress in the workplace can impact our well-being, morale, performance at work, and, most importantly, our personal lives, and by extension, our friends, and families.

When the 'Black Dog' of depression arrived for me, I did not realise what was happening. The website www.betterhelp.com describes the impact perfectly:

'The black dog of depression represents the gradual overtaking of the things you once loved, the person you once recognised in the mirror, or the life you once lived. Depression does not take breaks but instead follows you around like a shadow – a large, lumbering shadow, loyal as a canine.'

In my case, workplace conflict was a more insidious form of bullying and harassment.

The term 'gaslighting' means that the perpetrator(s) strategy is to cause the victim to believe that they are misinterpreting the situation in which they find themselves. The victim also comes to believe that they are directly responsible for the awful situation.

It seems unbelievable. However, I can vouch for the fact that this bizarre situation actually happens, because it happened to me! I thought that I was at the top of my game as a police Inspector. I felt good about work and life. My Professional Development Reviews

(PDRs) were very favourable. I had been told by a senior line manager that a strategic project would confirm my suitability for promotion to Chief Inspector.

I had been a project manager in my police organisation for a national piece of work. There were five other police forces piloting this. All of us had the scope to devise for our own organisations how we would engage stakeholders, both internally and externally.

In essence, the work concerned an ongoing topical question as to how to improve and regularise how police interact with minority communities. Their experience of policing was not as positive as it should have been.

I must admit, although you will be surprised to hear me say it, that despite being a very experienced operational officer, I was unaware of the depth and extent of the disquiet felt by the delivery of policing to young people and minority communities in Hertfordshire.

I wasn't an ignoramus, but I assumed that all was well in my borough and county. I thought the problems lay elsewhere. How wrong I was!

I am describing the context in such detail because the importance of leadership in conflict resolution is well-established in my mind. In other words, I was a confident individual. Everything in the garden seemed rosy as we say in the United Kingdom.

The horrific reality that brought me into a very dark place was about to reveal itself in excruciating ways that I could never have imagined.

Even worse was that I did not recognise this reality. It was to take an intervention by my doctor during a routine check-up for me to understand what untrammeled, insidious bullying, amplified by vicious micromanagement, could do to me and had done to me.

I concentrate in this narrative on my psychological state and how it changed. Externally, I had brought community representatives into the heart of the project, as they had developed links with the police that would improve trust and confidence in policing. Internally, I had won the support of the Command Teams of every business unit in the organisation. They told me that they would actively support the implementation of the changes to the maximum extent possible.

I reported to a Chief Inspector, who was the Project Lead, and the Deputy Chief Constable, who was the Executive Lead. Both were strong supporters of my work.

Just as the changes were being implemented, we had a change of Chief Constable. In effect, he was the Chief Executive Officer of the police organisation in which I served.

I had seen correspondence from him, in his previous role as Deputy Chief Constable in another organisation, to the Home Office, where he had consistently sought to undermine the project as 'bureaucratic nonsense'. Nonetheless, I felt certain that with the hierarchy of my organisation being so supportive of the project, he would be more receptive than hitherto. I could not have been more wrong.

Soon after his arrival, the new Chief Constable convened a meeting with the Deputy Chief Constable, Chief Inspector, and me in his office meeting room. The subject was the implementation of the project.

The police are a very hierarchical organisation. 'Command and Control' remains the culture to this day. The default position is that a person of a higher rank speaks, and subordinates only respond if invited to do so.

The Chief Constable opened the meeting by saying: **'The only reason we are doing this project is because a few dark people complain.'**

I was stunned.

The comments were racist and ignorant of the facts. He was known to be an arrogant individual, who brooked no challenges. The room was silent.

The Deputy Chief Constable looked down at the table. He was known to be a strong character and had earned the nickname of 'Basher' in the organisation. He stayed silent.

The Chief Inspector was doodling on a message pad. He remained silent.

I could not remain silent. I was regarded in the organisation as a maverick. That is, I spoke up and challenged errant behaviours. I felt compelled to speak.

This was the one time in my 34 years that I uttered the immortal words, 'With the greatest of respect, Chief Constable. You are wrong.'

I explained why he was so grievously wrong to say what he had said. The silence was deafening.

The Chief Constable looked furious. He went white. His eyes bulged. He clearly did not take kindly to being challenged, particularly by a mere Inspector. The meeting then broke up. Interestingly, there were no instructions concerning the project.

Outside the room, the Chief Inspector said, "That is our careers finished." How perceptive he was to be proved. I was to be collateral damage.

The following day, the Chief Constable defined his character in a dramatic manner. He presented the annual Policing Plan at the Grove Hotel, Watford. This is a five-star place. Very prestigious. The audience consisted of Members of Parliament, councillors, community representatives, and the hierarchy of the organisation.

The Chief Constable delivered death by PowerPoint.

When he came to the slide entitled 'Diversity', it read: *the golden thread that runs through policing*. He said, 'Never just the legal minimum!' There are no polite words to describe this hypocritical, bullying, racist.

He was presenting to the audience that he was personally committed to ensuring maximum adherence to the principles of Equality, Diversity, and Inclusion. (EDI)

The Deputy Chief Constable left to join another force by way of promotion.

The revenge of the Chief Constable on me was about to begin.

Within a month there was a promotion process for Chief Inspector. I collated my evidence and submitted it via the Chief Inspector. Feedback from a Superintendent, who was my second-line manager, was that some of my evidence was at the level expected of a Superintendent. He was not given to hyperbole or currying favour with junior ranks, so I was quietly confident of passing the initial 'sift' which failed candidates whose evidence was deemed below the required standard.

Unfortunately, my evidence was deemed to have been below standard for progressing to the interview stage by one mark. Initially, I thought this was by way of a shot across my bows after the encounter with the Chief Constable.

Three months later, which was most unusual, there was another promotion process. In the meantime, I honed and polished my evidence so that it sparkled!

I should add that when applying for promotion, the positive support of each line manager was required to pass to the next person. Only if the head of the business unit gave their approval would the application proceed to the central promotion board.

Unfortunately, again my evidence was deemed deficient by one mark for me to progress to the interview stage. Marcellus in Hamlet would have said, 'Something is rotten in the state of Denmark.' I had to agree.

What was going to be the next turn of the screw designed to break me? I did not have long to wait for the answer.

The support from the Senior Leadership Teams in each of the various business units began to visibly melt away. Prearranged appointments to discuss the implementation plan of the project were cancelled. People were 'too busy' to reschedule. Data sharing and reports were scanty and short of detail. Requests for more detailed feedback were ignored. People who were previously keen to share a coffee with me and 'shoot the breeze' began to make excuses.

I was being shunned. In Soviet terms, I was becoming a Zek or 'nonperson'.

I made all sorts of excuses in my mind for these events. I did not want to believe what was happening to me.

The Chief Inspector moved back to his home area to avoid the increasingly toxic atmosphere. He suggested that I do the same. However, I was so passionate and committed to the potential for change that would lead to a better form of policing that I thought I could tough it out.

Since the implementation had begun, the Executive of the organisation had requested an executive summary of activity for the preceding week. There was always feedback and comments received from them. I incorporated their suggestions into daily business. Once the replacement Chief inspector arrived, things changed radically.

He said, "I'm unsighted on what you send to the Exec. Please copy me in before you send it to the Exec."

I did so.

He then took to emailing me his suggested changes. The changes were coloured red. It was just like being back at school. He sat opposite me behind a screen on the table we shared. Rather than speak, he emailed me!

He would send the 'authorised version' to the Executive. What was in the report he submitted weekly; I had no idea. He shared nothing.

I had become a zek, a prisoner in the gulag. I had begun to dread going to work. I kept wondering where the next blow to my professional pride would fall. I felt too ashamed to speak to anyone. I thought I must be imagining things.

Matters came to a head one day when I saw my doctor for a routine check-up. She was shocked at my condition. Because she knew me and with her professional expertise, she diagnosed me as suffering from extreme stress. In all the situations I had been in the police, I had always been able to manage my stress levels. Clearly not this time!

The point to note is that I was a very confident professional person who did not recognise that what was happening to me was an insidious form of bullying.

I was certified sick with stress for six weeks. I hated following the medical instruction but accepted it was for the best. I received excellent pastoral support from a friend, who was a senior colleague from another police organisation.

I began to appreciate that what had happened to me was not just wrong but unlawful. We discussed my options. I wanted the bullying to stop and to return to work doing what I loved – leading people.

I felt that it was important to draw a line in the sand to protect myself, so I raised a Grievance. I had no idea about the procedure. I spent a considerable amount of time writing out the particulars across some twenty sides of A4.

Doing so was horrible, reliving each escalation in the order in which they had occurred. At the same time, it was cathartic for my soul and well-being.

Whilst I was away the implemented structure was removed. The senior management buy-in had evaporated. It was as if the project was an illusion, a figment of my imagination. Clearly, the community representatives and the wider groups had a different view.

I remember the feeling I had when I handed over the printed report, attached to the grievance form, to my new line manager. It was a combination of trepidation mixed with exhilaration. It was like I was literally divesting myself of a burden. My grievance was directed at the Chief Inspector because of his direct behaviour towards me.

I felt that it would prove to be impossible for me to prove the culpability of the Chief Constable for what had happened to me. Would all those Chief Superintendents, Superintendents, and Chief Inspectors who comprised the Command Teams be willing to risk their careers for me by telling the truth? I thought not.

I did not trust the staff association to do right by me. Therefore, I insisted that I be accompanied and supported by my professional senior colleague, whom I trusted, rather than someone I did not know personally.

We met with the new Deputy Chief Constable. He said, 'I've never read anything like this in my life. When I got to the bottom of each page, I wondered what I would find on the next page.'

He then said, 'Firstly, I must apologise to you for what you've suffered. It is inexcusable.'

The corporate apology was very important to me.

I felt vindicated that I hadn't imagined or overreacted to what had been done to me.

The Deputy Chief Constable asked me what I wished to get out of the process. I said not to be bullied; I wanted to be treated fairly. I got my wish, but I never sought further promotions.

You may think, *why not just transfer to another police organisation?* I had no confidence in the organisation to permit either of these outcomes whilst the Chief Constable was in place.

I should add that the grievance procedure materials are all in a bright orange box file in my loft. Since placing it there, I have never opened it. There is a folder entitled 'Grievance' on my laptop. I have never clicked on it since meeting the Deputy Chief Constable. Even seeing the folder when I scroll down on my laptop screen causes me to have the most awfully negative feelings. I was traumatised and to an extent I still am. This is what workplace conflict can do to people.

Wider lessons

Should I have pressed to have my promotion applications reassessed? That is something I have struggled with for a long time.

I just wanted the pain to end and resume doing what I loved to do – learning and leading people to develop to their maximum and find their own fulfilment of purpose.

In the context of the value of managers understanding their reports as people, rather than a role, I trust that I have demonstrated in a vivid fashion how a grievance procedure and the upholding of that grievance is a pyrrhic victory. The damage to trust and confidence in the organisation may be irreparable.

Grievance procedures are invariably, win-lose or lose-lose – unlike workplace mediation, which is a win-win. This is because fractured relationships can be repaired by workplace mediation and the participants design their own positive way forward.

Ideally, if the organisation that I was a member of had had a culture of using workplace mediation, what a difference that could have made to my professional and personal life.

If the Chief Constable and I could have had our conflict resolved by participating in mediation, then the benefits would have been immense for him, me, and the organisation.

Managers have a great deal to gain, or lose, by investing the time to understand the people they are responsible for. This can create trust and confidence in the 'difficult conversations' that are needed from time to time.

Effective and appropriate early intervention by the manager is key to developing a healthy work culture.

For managers to have the necessary skill and expertise to understand what is required of them, organisations must invest in the development of their managers' skill set, often described as Continuous Professional Development (CPD), and provide effective support that is structured, and professional guidance as appropriate from HR and senior managers.

It is a truism that what got you there won't get you to where you want to be.

Chapter Six

My Epiphany
A Complex Mediation successfully conducted by Anthony Munday
As told by
Mina Parmar, CEO, Assured HR

'In 2020, I was a governor of a school in the London Borough of Harrow. I had been selected as the Chair of the Grievance Panel, because of my significant experience in HR at both a strategic and operational level. The effectiveness of the Senior Leadership Team (SLT) at the school had been heavily compromised for several years. There had been significant workplace conflict involving the Head Teacher, Deputy Head, and several other members of the SLT.

'The impact upon the school, other colleagues, and the brand reputation of the school can be imagined. All had previously been friends until one was appointed Head Teacher. Personal and professional relationships had broken down.

'There had been a series of grievances alleging bullying by the Head Teacher. The grievances had not been upheld. Cases had been lodged with the Employment Tribunal. People had been conditioned. Some of them had had periods of absence from work, citing stress. Staff Association representatives were required to support those feeling stressed. Communication between them became extremely formal and was executed mostly by email.

"I recommended mediation as an intervention to break the cycle of toxicity. Other governors were sceptical of the chances of success. I explained that I knew a very experienced mediator who had a proven track record of dealing successfully with complex issues. I was aware of the unique 'icebreaker stage' that Anthony Munday had developed to create authentic trust and confidence in him as a mediator.

'Anthony met with the six individuals and created the environment to move forward to the formal stages of mediation. So successful had he been in creating that necessary trust and confidence in him as a mediator that, of the six persons who had been scheduled to be supported by staff association specialists, all felt that they were sufficiently confident not to do so.

'Anthony facilitated the creation of a Written Agreement between the participants.

Albeit a confidential document, they wished the document shared with the Board of Governors and the entire SLT.

'I witnessed the powerful and positive impact of Anthony Munday as a mediator dealing with a complex situation. The challenge faced by mediators in creating rapport, trust, and confidence with participants is overcome by his unique 'icebreaker stage'. Anthony deserves wider recognition for his innovatory ideas in mediation.'

Why Epiphany?

The Oxford Dictionary defines 'epiphany' as a sudden and surprising moment of understanding'.

My epiphany occurred in January 2020, just before the first Pandemic lockdowns in the UK.

Mina Parmar of Assured HR and I were discussing business development. She described a highly charged and complex conflict involving several members of the SLT of an Academy of which she was a Governor. She was the HR expert on the Board.

Mina described a very toxic culture that was impacting negatively on the SLT.

Five of the members of the SLT had submitted a series of grievances concerning the style and behaviours of the Headteacher. They alleged bullying and the three sets of grievances had not been upheld. The situation continued to deteriorate, so the Governing Body was considering dismissals of those who had raised grievances.

This drastic step had potentially significant consequences for the individuals, the SLT, and the organisation. There were implications for the brand reputation of the school.

Three different staff associations were involved in representing the six people and cases had been lodged with the Employment Tribunal.

Mina recalled my professional expertise as a workplace mediator and advised the Board of Governors of my availability to assist them to solve a seemingly intractable problem.

Her request for my services was like a bolt out of the blue, a true epiphany.

My experience of developing rapport with victims, witnesses, and suspects was my foundation for mediation. I found a highly charged and complex set of circumstances that had become deeply ingrained among the participants.

The concept of the pre-mediation meeting or 'icebreaker' was, of course, unknown to both the direct participants and the representatives of the three staff associations. Once I had explained the rationale of this unique stage and how it would be conducted, it was warmly received by them all.

My active listening skills and knowledge of NLP assisted me to appreciate the extent of the trauma that I was dealing with.

Since I left the police force some ten years previously, my business focus was on business development. I worked with clients, facilitating them to become leaders in their businesses and to understand and practice a coaching style of leadership rather than command and control.

The other aspect that I took a keen interest in, was for them to genuinely understand the difference between working in the business and working on the business.

Working in the business was narrow-focused. It often focuses on tactical aspects of the performance of tasks by others, or which could usefully and properly be delegated to others, or aspects that they were not passionate about.

Similarly, employing people to undertake tasks mostly to 'keep it in the family' was not necessarily the most productive use of time.

Work-Life Balance had meaning.

These challenges were magnified as many of my clients were SMEs. The business owner had a skill and created a business based on that expertise. Unfortunately, running a business was another matter.

Working on the business was more strategic, both in how to develop the business and their professional skill set.

It was an honour for me to create that rapport, trust, and confidence with the business owners so that I accessed the person and not their role. This aspect became increasingly significant to me; far more so than the numbers associated with the business plan.

It became evident to me that the simple truths described in the following quote by Steve Jobs applied to me:

'Your time is limited, so don't waste it living someone else's life. Don't be trapped by dogma, which is living with the results of other people's thinking. Don't let the noise of other's opinions drown out your own inner voice. And most important, have the courage to follow your heart and intuition. They somehow already know what you truly want to become. Everything else is secondary.'

Chapter Seven

The Chrysalis Method of Conflict Resolution
Stage One – Pre-Mediation Meeting or 'Icebreaker'.

Introduction

The website of ACAS defines themselves thus :

The Advisory, Conciliation, and Arbitration Service (ACAS) is a Crown non-departmental public body of the Government of the United Kingdom. Its purpose is to improve organisations and working life through the promotion and facilitation of strong industrial relations practices.

My model was developed from two sources.

My experiences as a trained mediator whilst in the police revealed the extreme challenges faced by internal mediators.

Chief among them was the issue of trust and confidence in my neutrality, fairness, objectivity, and fairness. I was understandably regarded as being a member of 'management', being an Inspector.

This concern was also reflected in extreme concern about the confidentiality of the process. Pretty much everyone in the organisation, including me, strongly believed with good reason that HR stood for 'Human Remains'.

HR was seen as a department that empowered managers to deliver bad news with the minimum legal consequences for the organisation. This may have been harsh, or unfair, but that was seen as the grim reality.

The second source of my training as a mediator was a much more positive experience, namely a five-day course in workplace mediation with ACAS in 2021. This was subject to external accreditation by the Northern Council for Further Education (NCFE). The course was intense and enjoyable. I was proud and relieved that my submitted answers to six randomised questions were of the required standard. Each answer was at least 1,000 words.

The Course was pass or fail. My answers to the questions were rigorously assessed to examine my suitability for confirmation as an ACAS-accredited mediator.

The certificate is proudly displayed on my LinkedIn profile and my website at
www.maverickmediator.co.uk

The Civil Mediation Council (CMC) has a robust process for registration to become a CMC-approved workplace mediator.

I successfully evidenced my capability and became registered in 2021. 'CMC workplace mediator' sits proudly on my LinkedIn profile too.

Delivering Tranquillity out of Trauma

The logo for my business 'The Maverick Mediator' was created and chosen with care and deliberation as you'd expect.

The leaves symbolise peace and tranquillity.

The two hands intertwined symbolise a firm agreement cemented in trust and confidence.

'Delivering tranquillity' is coloured green, symbolising positive energy, and looking forward.

'Out of trauma' is coloured red, symbolising negative energy, looking backward.

Stage One. The Pre-mediation meeting or 'Icebreaker'

Trauma is a very strong word in my opinion.

The Oxford definition is very pertinent to mediation:

'… a mental condition caused by severe shock, stress, or fear, especially when the harmful effects last for a long time.'

My experience is that participants suffer significant pain, distress, and trauma as a direct result of months, sometimes years, of workplace conflict.

In the workplace context, the cost of conflict is shared by their families, friends, colleagues, and the wider organisation.

No one goes to work to have a bad day.

The costs include absenteeism, sickness from stress, presenteeism, or 'quiet quitting'. This term means those people who turn up for work but are going through the motions. They are present in the body but not in their soul. They may be seriously considering looking for another position within the organisation or looking outside the organisation.

Their engagement with the mission statement will be perfunctory at best.

Productivity will be reduced, and thus the profitability of the organisation.

The considerable cost of recruiting to replace experienced personnel is another aspect to be considered. The productivity curve of new members of staff will be less than that of experienced personnel.

The other area that suffers is the private lives of participants.

The 'crossover effect' from work to private life can then translate into the 'spillover effect'. This is when our psyche and mood based on our workplace set the tone and characterises our dealings with friends and family and others in our private lives.

Visually, this is akin to when we drop a stone into still water. The ripples extend much further than we may think. The analogy isn't exactly as the ripples are visible. The impact of trauma at work can be disguised to ourselves and our nearest and dearest.

I know, that is what happened to me.

It is not a nice place to be. In respect of the workplace, traumatised people can disguise or minimise the impact on themselves, to others, as well as themselves.

When I am advised by a client organisation of a need for my professional services as a mediator, I do not require their perspective on the dispute. I only need to know the contact email addresses of the participants. This is necessary to ensure that attendance for the mediation process is voluntary and that I am not tainted by another's subjective view of the participants.

Thus, when I meet the participants for the first time, in the 'icebreaker', my perspective is objective and clean. The psychological state I see them in is highly instructive. This extends to body language, non-verbal communication, and how they speak.

Subsequently, what they say, how they say it, and what they don't say, become the baseline for me to evaluate our journey of authentic rapport, together.

The saying goes that 'You only get one chance to make a first impression'.

This is the crux of why this pre-mediation process is so important.

Between the participant and I, we are strangers meeting for the first time. How we create and develop that authentic rapport between us, unencumbered with diving into the matters that are to be mediated cannot be underestimated in its importance, for the whole process.

My approach is to have a laser-like focus on all the clues, verbal and non-verbal, visual and non-visual, without creating the feeling for the traumatised participant that they are being interrogated.

I signpost by initial email my mediation process so as to promote understanding, confidence, and trust in the process.

In my experience, the traumatic state of a participant can be exacerbated by their previous experience of mediation.

Here is an example of why this matters.

A participant presented herself in an almost petrified state.

She was a senior manager.

When I asked the question about her previous experience with mediation, she visibly tensed and replied.

"I am 34 years old. When I was 17, I was being mercilessly bullied at school.

The Head Teacher said that he would mediate."

"What happened?" I asked.

"The Head took the bully and me to his office. We sat opposite each other, and he sat in the corner.

For an hour the bully shouted and swore at me. The Head remained silent and inert.

After an hour, the Head looked at his watch and said 'That's enough. The Mediation is over."

I asked, "What happened next"?

She replied "We went outside, and the bully beat me up.

For 17 years I had thought that this was mediation. I was terrified that this would happen to me all over again.

Thank you so much for helping me to understand how what I had endured was not mediation."

She visibly relaxed and was smiling as she spoke.

Just imagine if I followed the process of every other mediator, and met her for the first time at the next stage, the Individual Meeting.

Location

The venue chosen must be neutral for all participants, ideally totally unconnected with their organisation, or at least geographically neutral from their place of work.

It should feel warm and professional.

Confidentiality for the participants must be guaranteed. The ambiance should be one of discretion.

I have found that a location such as a golf club is eminently suitable.

The room itself should be one where conversation between us can flow freely.

Top Tips

- Empathise with the participant.
- The Cambridge Dictionary defines 'empathy' as 'the **ability to share someone else's feelings or experiences by imagining what it would be like to be in that person's situation.**'
- Active Listening.
- The 6 techniques defined by the Center for Creative Leadership, www.ccl.org
  The description of the techniques refers to coaching. In my experience, Active Listening skills are as relevant to mediators as they are to Leaders.

1. Pay attention.

One goal of active listening and being an effective listener is to set a comfortable tone that gives your coachee an opportunity to think and speak. Allow 'wait time' before responding. Don't cut coachees off, finish their sentences, or start formulating your answer before they've finished. Pay attention to your body language as well as your frame of mind when engaging in active listening. Be focused on the moment, make eye contact, and operate from a place of respect as the listener.

2. Withhold judgment.

Active listening requires an open mind. As a listener and a leader, be open to new ideas, new perspectives, and new possibilities when practicing active listening. Even when good listeners have strong views, they suspend judgment, hold any criticisms, and avoid interruptions like arguing or selling their point right away.

3. Reflect.

When you're the listener, don't assume that you understand the other person correctly — or that they know you've heard them. Mirror your companion's information and emotions by periodically paraphrasing key points. Reflecting is an active listening technique that indicates that you and your counterpart are on the same page.

For example, your companion might tell you, *'Emma is so loyal and supportive of her people — they'd walk through fire for her. But no matter how much I push, her team keeps missing deadlines.'*

To paraphrase, you could say, *'So, Emma's people skills are great, but accountability is a problem.'*

If you hear, *'I don't know what else to do!'* or *'I'm tired of bailing the team out at the last minute,'* try helping your companion label their feelings: *'Sounds like you're feeling pretty frustrated and stuck.'*

4. Clarify.

Don't be shy to ask questions about any issue that's ambiguous or unclear when engaging in active listening. As the listener, if you have doubt or confusion about what your colleague has said, say something like, *'Let me see if I'm clear. Are you talking about ...?'* or *'Wait a minute. I didn't follow you.'*

Open-ended clarifying and probing questions are important active listening tools that encourage the colleague to do the work of self-reflection and problem-solving, rather than justifying or defending a position, or trying to guess the 'right answer'.

Examples include: *'What do you think about ...?'* or *'Tell me about ...?'* and *'Will you further explain/describe ...?'*

When engaging in active listening, the emphasis is on asking, rather than telling. It invites a thoughtful response and maintains a spirit of collaboration.

You might say: *'What are some of the specific things you've tried?'* or *'Have you asked the team what their main concerns are?'* or *'Does Emma agree that there are performance problems?'* and *'How certain are you that you have the full picture of what's going on?'*

5. Summarise.

Restating key themes as the conversation proceeds confirms and solidifies your grasp of the other person's point of view. It also helps both parties to be clear on mutual responsibilities and follow-up. Briefly summarise what you've understood while practicing active listening, and ask the other person to do the same.

Giving a brief restatement of core themes raised by the colleague might sound like: *'Let me summarise to check my understanding. Emma was promoted to manager, and her team loves her. But you don't believe she holds them accountable, so mistakes are accepted and keep happening. You've tried everything you can think of, and there's no apparent impact. Did I get that right?'*

Restating key themes helps <u>increase accountability</u>.

6. Share.

Active listening is *first* about understanding the other person, *then* about being understood as the listener. As you gain a clearer understanding of the other person's perspective, you can begin to introduce your own ideas, feelings, and suggestions. You might talk about a similar experience you had or share an idea that was triggered by a comment made previously in the conversation.

Once the situation has been talked through in this way, both you and your colleague have a good picture of where things stand. From this point, the conversation can shift into problem-solving: *What hasn't been tried? What don't we know? What new approaches could be taken?*

As the coach, continue to query, guide, and offer, but don't dictate a solution. Your colleague will feel **more confident and eager if** they think through the options and own the solution.

Used in combination, these six active listening techniques are the keys to holding a coaching conversation and, similarly, an effective mediation session.

The key benefit of this stage is that the participant and I do not meet as strangers at the Individual Meeting, as is the case with other forms of workplace mediation.

I know that other mediators regard an initial telephone conversation with participants as a suitable and effective method to develop trust and confidence in the process.

Not for me.

The interests of the participant are paramount to me.

I evidence this fact by the allocation of at least an hour for the participant and me to create authentic rapport.

Chapter Eight

The Chrysalis Method of Conflict Resolution: Stage Two
The Individual Meeting

The Individual Meeting is where other workplace mediators would meet the participant for the first time.

Note, that I use the term 'participant', which is less adversarial than the legal term 'party'.

I have demonstrated in the previous chapter the benefit of the Pre-Mediation Meeting (PMM) or 'icebreaker' for participants and myself as the mediator, to develop the necessary authentic rapport, including trust and confidence in the process and myself.

Feedback from participants is that they want a system whereby they meet a mediator, develop trust and confidence in them, and the process is challenging. At best, they advise me that they engage with the mediator at a more superficial level than if they had not experienced the Pre-Mediation Meeting (PMM).

A combination of the PMM and. Ideally, the two-day interval we agree before the Individual Meeting is invaluable for participants. Bearing in mind that invariably participants are traumatised by long periods of conflict before I meet them, they have a lot to process. A combination of the PMM and the time interval before the Individual Meeting enables them to dive deep into the issues and be more aware of the opportunity to discuss their core issues at a deeper level.

Another area of difference for my model is that I consider in-person mediation far more powerful and relevant for traumatised participants.

Workplace mediation is a confidential process. This cannot be guaranteed by the use of online platforms. Simply put, it is impossible to know who is out of sight of the camera.

The integrity of the process is also compromised by the virtual mediation process in my view. It becomes more of a task that we can engage with to the extent we choose, more readily when online than in person.

Being present means exactly that.

In the Individual Meeting, participants can be provided with pastoral support from a friend or staff association representative. This is a common feature with other processes concerning workplace conflict, such as a grievance procedure.

I adopt a slightly different perspective from the ACAS model. I invite the supporting person to play a fuller, more proactive role during the Individual Meeting. My reasoning is that the best interests of the traumatised participant are at the heart of the mediation process. I confirm with the participant that they have trust and confidence in the capability of the supporting person to add value and purpose to the mediation. In the presence of both the participant and supporting person, I signpost how the meeting will be conducted and its purpose.

I explain that in effect, we are all members of a team whose mission is to ensure that the participant's story is fully told. If the supporting person has a point to make that will assist in the uncovering of a pertinent fact that will enhance the fullest exposure of the story, they are encouraged to speak up. This is not by way of advocacy, speaking on behalf of the participant, but to add detail, flavour, and context in a way that the participant may have inadvertently neglected to do.

When the participant has fully described their perspective on the workplace conflict, I signpost them about the next stage in the process, the Joint Meeting.

Feedback from participants at the conclusion of the Individual Meeting is that they have felt confidence and trust in me to describe their perspective at a deeper interest level, rather than at a superficial positional level, which would have been the case without the PMM.

The time they have had since the PMM has enabled them to reflect on what the conflict is about for them.

Participants are adamant that we would not have discussed their perspective in the depth that we had if there had been no PMM and interval before our Individual Meeting.

One of the biggest challenges of the Individual Meeting is the fear and trepidation felt by participants at facing each other in the same room. These concerns can be amplified when the dynamics of power are at play. In the Individual Meeting, I explain how those concerns can best be resolved for the benefit of all participants.

In conjunction with each participant, we draw up a list of ground rules that are designed and intended to ensure an environment of respectful listening during the Joint Meeting.

The rules are created and agreed upon with each participant in their individual meeting.

The consolidated list is agreed upon at the start of the Joint Meeting.

The following rules are shown by way of example:

- The mediator will create an agenda based on the order of participant presentations.
- Participants will each be provided with between 5–10 minutes to present their perspectives to the others.
- There will be no interruptions by any of the participants to the presentation by each of the participants.
- The language used by participants will always be appropriate and respectful of each other.
- All participants will actively listen to the other presentations.
- All participants will be patient whilst others present their perspectives to the meeting.
- Non-verbal communication will also adhere to the principle of mutual respect.
- The mediator will summarise the issues raised in the presentation. The participant will confirm the accuracy and fairness of the summary.

- Once all participants have delivered their presentation, the mediator will summarise the issues.
- The mediator will then create a balanced agenda that meets the needs of all participants.

It should be said not all workplace mediations are between two people. My principal area of focus is conflicted, senior teams. I have mediated up to seven people during a single process.

A contrast with arbitration is that I emphatically do not convey to each participant what others have said in an attempt to seek common ground. That is not the role of the mediator. It can be challenging when specific events are described by each participant from their individual perspective. Nonetheless, the role and responsibility of the mediator are to develop the necessary trust and confidence in each participant so that an atmosphere is created for them to share their deep-seated perspective on their interests.

Rapport, trust, and confidence in both the mediation process and me, is not achieved by having a pre-set bank of questions that are fired at each participant. Remember, I know only what the participants are comfortable sharing with me. I actively listen to what is said, how it is said, and what is not said. This requires intense concentration on my part. However, the ambiance that I create must never feel judgemental or intrusive to any of the participants.

Equally important is that I do not refer to anything said in the Individual Meeting of one participant to another. At the same time, I am not interviewing suspects engaged in a joint enterprise, looking to catch people out with inconsistencies. Similarly, it is extremely important that I do allow anything said in one Individual Meeting to prejudice my neutrality, fairness, objectivity, and impartiality; in another Individual Meeting.

Here is a recent example that will serve to illustrate these points.

The two participants were senior union officials. Behaviours and comments in the workplace by them, to and about each other provided a toxic cocktail for others.

Over the course of five years in the same organisation, the culture had become like a sporting fixture. Both the participants, in effect, had created teams of supporters who behaved towards them when they were in the same zone as if supporting opposing teams. These behaviours included chanting about the merits of each of the participants as the mood took them.

The participants both played to the gallery, thus making matters worse for the workforce and organisation. In other words, their conflict had become a ritual. This was to the detriment of the organisation, their teams, the participants, and their families.

Interestingly, my client was the staff association rather than the organisation that employed them! The staff association was in despair at the impact on their brand reputation and smooth working of their own organisation.

The background that emerged during the Individual Meetings was interesting.

The participants were neighbours and former friends. They had played golf together, enjoyed family barbecues, and went on holiday together. They had climbed the ladder of the organisation and the staff association in a similar fashion. So, what had caused the rupturing of their relationship?

Some **five years** earlier, one participant had sent a cryptic WhatsApp message to the other as a joke. The recipient said nothing but was incensed. He made excuses to his family as to why he was no longer friends with the other person.

Since the men had fallen out, this spilled over to the families. They became estranged from each other, and the situation deteriorated so that contact and communication between them were the bare minimum.

The impact of the WhatsApp message remained unbeknown to each other until the Joint Meeting!

In the Individual Meeting with the recipient, they spoke at length about it. Until that meeting, I was the first person to learn of the true impact of the message.

If I was an arbitrator, when I met the second participant for their Individual Meeting, I would have raised this straightaway, looking to achieve a positive result. However, I was not an arbitrator but a mediator. It was not my professional responsibility to direct the thinking of the participant who had sent the message as to its direct significance.

As a mediator, my responsibility is to create a safe space where the second participant provided their fullest perspective on the conflict. They had no conception as to what was behind the falling out.

The Individual Meeting(s) enables me as the mediator to gauge how far people have come, psychologically, since the PMM. Since we are not strangers to each other and have an authentic rapport with each other, the meeting provides a 'divesting of stress' for the participant. They are speaking, often for the first time, about the core interests that underpin their concerns.

If trust and confidence are not there, then conversations would be at a superficial level at best, and at their position level.

In my experience, I have mediated between participants who over a period of two years have raised grievances about bullying and harassment by a manager and their conversations have remained at a superficial level.

In this case, there had been a series of three grievances raised by several members of a Senior Leadership Team (SLT). The grievances were investigated internally, as per policy, and were found to be unproven.

Such outcomes benefited neither the people concerned nor their organisation. Relationships continued to deteriorate to the extent that several members of the SLT would only communicate with the CEO via email.

The HR Director believed termination of employment for several senior staff was the preferred option. The option of mediation was then discussed, and I was requested to assist.

In the Individual Meetings, I learned that all the participants were former friends. Several had applied for the position of CEO. Once one was promoted, relationships deteriorated alarmingly, as previously described.

During these meetings, it became evident that the CEO believed they had to be seen to be adopting a 'no favourites or friends' style of management. There was no mentoring support for the CEO. It was up to them to learn on the job. The CEO was so concerned to be seen to be fair that she overcompensated in her dealings with her former friends.

They used to socialise together as a group but that fell away. It became a vicious downward spiral to the extent that individually, all were unhappy but could not find the words to say to each other over the preceding period.

In my role as a mediator, what is revealed in the Individual Meetings was confidential. It was not my place to suggest or lead people, based on what they did not know when I had other Individual Meetings.

In such cases, the first time that people in conflict can express themselves fully to each other is at the subsequent Joint Meeting.

Chapter Nine

The Chrysalis Method of Conflict Resolution
Stage Three – The Joint Meeting

This stage of the mediation process is the most stressful for participants and the mediator.

It is one thing to describe the impact and the detail of the conflict in an Individual Meeting with a mediator and with the physical support of a staff association representative or friend. It is quite another to do so in the direct presence of other participants with whom they are conflicted.

Whilst mediation is often seen as a conflict involving two participants, in practice, the number can vary. The largest number of participants I have facilitated in a specific mediation was six senior members of staff. They were formerly good friends.

Several of them had applied for the CEO position. One of this group was chosen and relationships began to suffer. It reached the stage that two of them refused to communicate with their former friend and CEO except via email. Trust between them had completely broken down. The fear of being in the same room was palpable.

In the preceding two years there had been three sets of grievances from five of the SLT members against alleged bullying behaviours by the CEO. None had been upheld. The culture had become increasingly toxic.

None of the people could be regarded as having 'won'. Indeed themselves, SLT colleagues, and the wider organisation could very easily be described as having 'lost'.

The Board was actively considering dismissals as their preferred option to resolve this conflict. The toxicity was infecting the culture and effective working of the SLT. However, the HR Director was aware of the benefits of mediation. The Board was persuaded to give this process a try since they were at their wits' end.

We shall return to these participants later in this chapter.

Online Mediation

Some mediators when liaising with clients, particularly after the lockdowns and 'Working from Home' during or after the pandemic, extol the virtues of online mediation. It is portrayed as being cost-effective and less intrusive in terms of abstraction of staff than in-person mediation. Clients are advised that they will not have to factor in the travelling costs of participants and the mediator. Other benefits are that they do not need to find and pay for another venue. Participants can participate from their workplace or offices within the organisation.

Workplace Mediation is a confidential process. Confidentiality cannot be guaranteed since it is impossible to confirm who else may be present off-camera.

The other significant downside of investing in online mediation is that the most critical aspect of the mediation is heavily compromised by this decision.

Workplace Mediation is fundamentally about conflict where relationships have broken down between colleagues, sometimes friends. It is invariably the situation that participants have either not been in the same room as each other, or, when they do so, conflict reignites.

Therefore, I contend that the evidence that conflicted colleagues can be both in the same room without conflict recurring and can work together in a positive manner is not met by an online mediation.

What message is being sent to participants by their organisation choosing this option?

Firstly, they are rarely asked for their view. When the mediation process is offered to them, they are provided with a fait accompli. This is how it is.

Secondly, in the context of a workplace conflict, are participants keen to appear to be 'rocking the boat'?

Thirdly, mediation is seen as a task to be juggled between other commitments.

Fourthly, how seriously is the psychological state of participants taken by the organisation in deciding that this choice of online mediation is appropriate?

In my view, in-person mediation at a neutral venue demonstrates to the participants that their organisation values them as people. It evidences that the organisation is probably willing to invest in their people. It also signifies an awareness of the importance of their well-being.

My experience is that sometimes participants are or have been absent through sickness, often cited as work-related stress.

Mediation can restore people to the workplace rather than losing them forever. The costs of recruitment, retraining, and the reduced productivity of newcomers can be considerable.

Mediation is not a 'task' to be juggled. It is a serious process that requires commitment from participants and their organisation. The psychology of traumatised people re-enacting behaviours that have caused conflict in the same buildings as their workplace is not a good starting point for mediation. The choice of a neutral venue reinforces trust by the participants in the regard with which their organisation takes their well-being seriously. For me, the choice of venue is vitally important. It should create the appropriate ambiance for traumatised people to relax and feel sufficiently positive so that they are encouraged to actively engage in the process.

Internal Mediators

I have a degree of direct personal experience with the challenges faced by people who are trained to the required quality standards as mediators but find they are not trusted by the participants.

In my police organisation I was trained to be a mediator. I mediated in different business units to my own, to appear 'independent' to the participants. I recognised the challenges of participants not seeing me as part of the management. They also found it difficult to believe that the essential confidentiality of the process would be respected. This is a serious challenge where trust and confidence in the organisation are at a low ebb. At best, I often believed that the participants engaged with the process at a superficial level.

Potential participants found it impossible to believe my personal assurances about the confidentiality of the process. They saw HR as a tool used by managers in the organisation to keep them in line. A truly shocking situation that meant that my personal professional credibility was subsumed, to the detriment of their engagement and trust in the mediation process.

I must admit that I could empathise with that viewpoint.

In most other aspects of organisational culture in the police force, Human Resources – who managed the process – were not trusted by people to respect confidentiality. Their prime loyalty was regarded as being to the organisation rather than people. Hence, they were referred to disparagingly as 'Human Remains'.

We all knew, or believed we knew, about the difference between the personal folder we could request to see, and the REAL folder, which contained all the juicy comments on us by people whom we had no opportunity to challenge.

It must be extremely challenging for Human Resources people who are qualified in mediation not to be trusted to respect the confidentiality that is essential to deliver successful outcomes.

The Joint Meeting

I have found that wearing business suits for mediation can convey the image of 'management', which would not be desirable.

I choose to wear smart casual clothing to indicate that it is not me as the mediator who is controlling this process. I am a part of the same team as the participants. I am there to facilitate the process. I do not OWN the process. The participants do.

One of the important considerations is the duration of the mediation process. I recognise the significance of the potential cost of abstraction for the client organisation.

The correct perspective is for the client organisation to recognise that it is investing in its people. It is also about demonstrating to the participants that words used on posters such as

'People are our greatest asset' are a statement of fact.

I am aware that some mediators (as part of their business offering) allocate one hour for the Initial Meeting (which includes their version of the 'icebreaker'), and two hours for the Joint Meeting.

My concerns are that whilst this may seem an appropriate use of valuable time, there are potential downsides. The time allocated may be insufficient. What then?

The participants and mediator are both focused on the time remaining instead of focusing on the problem. Setting an allotted time creates the same anticipation as an egg timer with the time depleting or an hourglass with the sand slowly piling up before your eyes.

This is clearly undesirable for all the obvious reasons.

By way of contrast, my allocated times are somewhat different:

- Pre-Mediation Meeting: 1.5 hours per participant
- Individual Meeting: 2 hours
- Joint Meeting: 6 hours

These are allocated hours.

We maximise the use of the available time. We do not sit idly but are not constricted by too challenging a time frame. In other words, time is not a driver towards a more superficial interaction by the participants. Rather, it provides sufficient time and space for the participants and me to achieve the purpose of each meeting.

In my preparations for the meetings at each stage, I arrive in good time at the venue to confirm that the facilities are to the required standard.

I have found that golf clubs are ideal for mediation. They are neutral and have an appropriate ambiance. They also provide the appropriate quality of meeting room and refreshments.

Other types of buildings can be used. Neutrality between the participants and the ambiance are the prerequisite characteristics that I consider. It must afford a 'safe space' for all participants.

In both the Individual and Joint Meetings, I have found it helpful to have available a flip chart to ensure that we have captured all the topics that the participant(s) wishes to discuss. Feedback from participants is a valuable way to ensure we have covered the topics of concern and interest in the meeting. It is also a graphical representation of the progress made. That is therapeutic for them. It also helps ensure that I do not inadvertently neglect a topic or not cover all the strands of discussion necessary.

When I welcome the participants, I congratulate them on their achievement in reaching this stage. They are not accompanied by pastoral support for this stage. The joint meeting is about creating a positive environment in which conflicted people can communicate with each other in a positive manner.

I signpost how the day will look. I reiterate the collective ground rules that have been agreed upon individually and check if there is anything missing for anyone. We then confirm that these are the ground rules that will apply for the Joint Meeting, ensuring a respectful environment.

We will then agree to the order in which each participant will present their impact statement to the meeting. I make a note of the relevant topics covered in the five-to-ten-minute presentation on the flipchart. This timeline is to ensure a clear focus on the most significant issues for each participant.

This is often the first time that the participants have had the opportunity to describe matters to each other in a respectful manner. Invariably, the reaction by the receiving person(s) is clearly impactive.

Whilst the person presenting describes their perspective of events, they often find it helpful for all participants that they describe how these events made them feel as people.

This can often be the first time that participants recognise each other as human beings rather than by the roles they occupy in the organisation.

On occasion, a participant may stray from the ground rules. I gently bring them back on track as to how we have agreed to conduct the joint meeting.

At the end of each presentation, I summarise what has been said including the pertinent issues. I check with the participant who has just presented to ensure accuracy. At the end of the presentations, we have an agreed list of topics for discussion. The agenda is then agreed upon by the participants.

For example, the topics of 'Communication' or 'Trust' may appear in more than one presentation. These are then grouped together for the subsequent discussion.

This is also a practical demonstration of conflicted colleagues working positively together, often for the first time in years.

Working through the agenda is perhaps the most emotionally charged part of the process. This is where the participants are actively and respectfully working together, facilitated by me, to ensure that the ground rules are observed.

The often-traumatic nature of events creates powerful responses. These include tears and apologies for behaviours between the participants as they discuss the matters at hand.

I'd previously described the group of six participants who had formerly been friends. During this part of the meeting, the shared apologies, tears, and horror at events were palpable.

The intensity of this shared experience was such that once completed, it was appropriate to break for lunch. I showed the group where to go for lunch. It was scheduled for 30 minutes. I had to respond to an urgent message that I had received earlier on my phone. Some minutes later, I returned to the group.

The laughter and sharing of photos of family on each other's phones was positive proof that their working together earlier was authentic and cathartic. It was a stunning testament to the positive potential of the mediation process. I naturally extended the lunch break until it reached its natural conclusion at 45 minutes.

The next part of the Joint Meeting is the creation of the Written Agreement. This is the document that is a form of a 'moral contract'. The participants, facilitated by me, work together to create a document that signifies how they will communicate together and their behaviours towards each other in the workplace. I use the term 'moral contract' because mediation is a confidential process. Nothing discussed during mediation can be referred to in any formal proceedings.

I write the agreement in the exact words required by the participants. When the participants are confident that the Written Agreement is complete, then it is signed and dated by the participants and me.

In effect, the participants have designed their own positive future for themselves. I facilitate but do not direct the conversations. The participants have sole responsibility to decide if the Written Agreement is to remain confidential or to be shared with specified persons for specified reasons. Such people include CEOs and HR heads. This is about sharing the success of joint working with people who have been most directly affected by workplace conflict.

Contingency

Experience has taught me that it can be valuable to agree on a contingency plan in case there is a failure of any part of the Written Agreement. This enables the group to re-assemble for a short time, usually a maximum of two hours. We then discuss what has happened, why it has happened, and how best to re-establish the relevant provisions of the Written Agreement.

I trust that you can see why I describe workplace mediation as a 'win-win'.

Chapter Ten

The Chrysalis Method of Conflict Resolution
Stage Four – The Review Meeting

Some mediators consider their responsibilities to their clients have concluded once the Joint Meeting has taken place or the Written Agreement has been written and shared as per the intentions of the participants.

I have adopted a fourth stage for my mediation process, which has been well received by both participants and client organisations, for reasons I will explain. When I am initially commissioned to undertake workplace mediation by a client organisation, I signpost the process including the review.

I explain that after one month of the Joint Meeting, I will conduct a Review Meeting with the participants.

Purposes

The purposes are threefold:
1. The participants: to confirm the status of the Written Agreement.

2. The participants discuss the core issues that contribute to conflict in the organisation.
3. The client organisation, HR Director, or HR Business Partner, to provide contemporary business intelligence on the data sets that pertain to conflict.

The participants

We have previously spoken of the contingency provision to enable participants and me to respond swiftly to breaches of the Written Agreement, thus keeping matters on track.

Experience has taught me that arranging to have the Review Meeting one month from the date of the Joint Meeting is about right for several reasons. It gives the participants a realistic timeframe to prove to themselves and each other that the terms of the Written Agreement they created are fair, realistic, and sustainable. Colleagues and participants can feel confident about the strength of the Written Agreement.

The wider organisation can regard the Written Agreement as embedded. The agreement becomes in effect 'business as usual'.

Families can enjoy having the best versions of the participants back with them in their private lives. This enables the participants to be at their best in the work context.

When I meet with the participants to review how the Written Agreement has operated, there is no preconception on my part. We work through each part of the agreement in sequence. Everyone is eager to contribute and give their perspective. The sharing of ideas and perspectives for a common purpose is the essence of teamwork.

Let me illustrate these concepts with a real-life example.

A group of five senior managers were participants in a mediation process. Their individual and collective behaviours towards each other over the preceding two years had been confined to their own organisation.

It was when this complex workplace conflict spilled over into professional meetings with other organisations that the ramifications became known to their CEO via senior people at those other organisations. This toxicity was now impacting the brand reputation of the client organisation.

The CEO had discussions with the HR Director. They considered instituting proceedings for Gross Misconduct with a view to dismissals as a very real potential outcome for some or all of the group.

The cost of business disruption would have been considerable for the organisation. The implications of the need for the recruitment of replacement staff and possible Employment Tribunals can well be imagined.

Fortunately, the CEO was meeting with other business associates concerning unconnected matters. During the meeting, the discussion moved on to workplace conflict. The benefits of workplace mediation were shared with the CEO, and I was commissioned to assist.

The participants I met at the Review Meeting had undergone a profound, positive change since I first met them at the Pre-Mediation Meeting. They had repaired their fractured relationships and challenging communication styles to become a cohesive team. It was fascinating and wonderful to see them demonstrating professional courtesy and consideration of each other's perspectives at the Review Meeting.

This is a key aspect for me.

The superficiality of engagement with the Review would become evident. What was happening was authentic and a powerful testament to the care, commitment, and thought that they had put into the mediation process. Their endeavours culminated in the creation of their Workplace Agreement. They were justly proud of how far they had come individually and as a team. The mediation process taught them the critical importance of emotional intelligence and active listening.

Postscript

About a year after this Review Meeting, I was in another business unit of the same organisation some 80 miles away conducting a mediation with two senior colleagues who were quite unconnected with the participants of the first group.

I had completed the first individual meeting and was on my lunch break. I was walking along a corridor when I noticed a woman, who smiled at me and said hello.

'Hello,' I said.

I must have looked non-plussed as she said, 'You don't recognise me, do you?'

I had to admit that she had the advantage over me. She took off her glasses and said, 'Does that help?'

I immediately recognised her as a participant from the previous mediation. She smiled broadly and said, without prompting,

'Thank you so much for what you did for us all. We are getting on really well. It is all thanks to you.'

She stretched out her hand and I shook it.

'Thank you again,' she said and then we parted. It was an unexpected but tangible indication of the power of workplace mediation.

The Client Organisation

Once we have reviewed the Written Agreement, we take a break for lunch. Experience tells me that this first part must not be rushed as it is an affirmation that a significant milestone has been achieved. It is not a 'tick box' exercise.

The second part of the review meeting is to ascertain from each participant, their perspective as to the core organisational issues and processes that contribute towards a propensity for workplace conflict. The business intelligence gleaned from each participant is bullet-pointed onto the ubiquitous flipchart.

When all participants have had their individual input, they have created a series of potential action points for their organisation. These are then prioritised by the group. Quite often, the participants have good ideas as to the causation factors.

All the intelligence is captured by me and a report for the client is prepared. The report is collated by me for the benefit of the client organisation. It is anonymised.

Meeting with HR Director or HR Business Partner

My meeting with a senior HR executive of the client organisation takes place afterward and is distinct from the participants.

In the month between the Joint Meeting and the Review Stage, I send a document to the HR Director or HR Business Partner which contains the following questions.

Data sets that may indicate workplace conflict.

1. What are your top three challenges in your organisation?

2. What makes them your top three challenges?

3. Do you have a stable headcount generally, except in any particular team?

4. Do you conduct any kind of exit interview?

5. If so, what themes are emerging about the team where there is high churn?

6. Is there high sickness absence in a team where it is known that conflict exists?

7. Not just a high incidence of coughs and colds, but absence for stress?

8. How many Employment Tribunals have been lodged in the past three years?

9. What have been the common themes of those Employment Tribunals?

10. What actions have been agreed upon to mitigate risks identified at those Employment Tribunals?

11. What system of confidential reporting of workplace concerns exists in the organisation?

12. What themes have emerged?

13. What are the numbers and patterns of Grievance Procedures telling you?

14. What are the numbers and patterns of Misconduct cases telling you?

15. What are the evidenced costs to the organisation of resignations and recruitment?

16. How could these costs be appropriately mitigated?

17. What is the nature and level of training for support for new managers in how to manage people effectively and fairly?

18. What Continuous Professional Development is provided for existing managers?

19. What system of Professional Development Review exists in the organisation?

20. What are the evidenced gaps in management training identified by the organisation?

21. What provision for Occupational Health exists in the organisation?

Such information gleaned from the participants and the organisation is of critical importance.

Benefits for the client organisation

The ability to have access to clean, unvarnished business intelligence is valuable and significant.

In effect, I have enabled the client organisation to utilise objectively sourced data to assist the process of organisational development. The impact on future workplace conflict is positive; the recognition of the impact of current methods of working, systems, and processes, leads to engagement and the retention of people.

Ultimately it is about equipping managers with the requisite skill set to manage people fairly and effectively.

The meeting with the HR executive will also include the CEO or Deputy CEO. We will discuss their opinion of the HR data sets and the perspective of the participants in terms of the management and mitigation of workplace conflict. This is a root cause analysis of conflict in their organisation.

We ascertain and determine the rationale for the attendees and the scope of questions for the next stage, the Structured Debrief.

Chapter Eleven

The Chrysalis Method of Conflict resolution.
Stage Five – Structured Debriefing

This stage flows naturally from the business intelligence gleaned from the second part of the review. The participants have provided their perspectives on the root causes of conflict within the client organisation. This is valuable intelligence but is not necessarily probative from a strategic perspective.

In essence, I am building a secure foundation of knowledge with the client to fully ascertain the nature and extent of workplace conflict.

The methodology I use to achieve this desirable situation is called Structured Debriefing. I am accredited in this expertise by both the National Police Improvement Agency (NPIA) and Centrex, and I have conducted debriefs at organisational, local, and national levels.

The overarching objective in this instance, is to gather the maximum amount of clean business intelligence from all relevant sources who will, in the debrief, share it amongst the attendees in an open and inclusive manner that will be captured by me. I will then create an Action Plan which consists entirely of the collective intelligence contributed by the attendees. This will propose priorities for organisation to act upon in their Implementation Plan.

Structured Debriefing is a timely and effective method to ensure that lessons are truly learned and a credible action plan that reflects this learning is produced.

Here is an overview of the process.

Phase One: Organisational Intelligence Gathering

- Meeting with the Senior Decision Maker (SDM) to clarify and confirm the points at issue, that will be subject to the Structured Debrief; this will include the nature and scope of the structured questions and the rationale for attendees.
- Confirmation of the Terms of Reference of the Structured Debrief.
- This will include the purpose, parameters, and procedure e.g., validation of each individual response to a question. There are no challenges permitted to each response.

- This is important when we consider the dynamics of power.

Phase Two: Organisational Intelligence Capture

- Delivery of the Structured Debrief: Digital Version or Immersive Version. Face-to-face is always preferable for the authenticity of the process.
- Consolidation of the business intelligence obtained (including emerging themes from the responses).
- Engage Partners for deeper assessments, as appropriate.
- Confirmation of the higher purpose of the Structured Debrief, including how the data obtained will inform the future strategy of the organisation.

Phase Three: Organisational Intelligence Enacted

- Delivery of the Action Plan founded upon the Structured Debrief.
- The Action Plan will confirm and clarify Organisational Priorities and Actions resulting directly from the Structured Debrief.

- Review of feedback from the client, including areas for improvement.
- Create an agreed timetable for the delivery of the Implementation Plan, Terms of Reference, Review, and Support with the Senior Decision Maker, to embed the cultural transformation.

Phase Four: Follow up and Review.

- Implementation of the Action Plan is the responsibility of the client organisation.
- Agree on a review timetable and schedule.
    - 3 Month
    - 6 Month
    - 12 Month
    - NB These dates are specified and agreed upon for our respective calendars.

My first meeting with the Senior Decision Maker is akin to my meeting a participant for the first time in the Pre-Mediation Meeting or 'icebreaker'.

In both cases, people are evaluating me on several levels. Our mutual objective is to create authentic rapport between us, sufficient to create the necessary trust and confidence in both me and the process.

In my experience, managers are fearful of structured debriefing for a few reasons:
- They believe that others, unlike themselves, are negative and resistant to change.
- They believe that others will have nothing new to contribute.
- They believe that they already know what others know.
- They believe that others will not take the process seriously.
- They believe that others will disrupt the process.
- They believe that they already know all there is to know about the subject matter of the debrief.
- They believe that others will be reluctant to provide their views.
- They believe that others are reluctant to take responsibility for the strategic direction of the organisation.
- They believe that others only know pertinent things about the business that are directly related to their role in the organisation.

- They believe that managers are already sufficiently and appropriately trained to manage people.
- They believe that others do not share their higher purpose perspective on the organisation.

These concerns are understandable, but experience teaches me that they are, for the most part, based upon a reflection of their existing leadership style and the culture of the organisation.

In that inaugural meeting at the Review Stage of the Chrysalis Method of Conflict Resolution, I actively seek out the concerns of the Senior Decision Maker and HR executives and seek to allay them.

I explain the protocols that will ensure the effective use of the valuable time of all attendees.

Typically, a Structured Debrief will last some two hours with twenty participants.

All attendees must validate their responses to the questions posed in the debrief, i.e., they must explain why something is important from their perspective.

There are no challenges permitted in the Structured Debrief

Together with my facilitation responsibilities, this ensures that the dynamics of power do not operate.

I explain that all attendees will be aware of the protocols beforehand. I reiterate them at the opening of the debrief.

The next order of business is to better understand the SDM as a leader and a person. This is essential because the full extent of the benefits of the Structured Debrief requires an understanding of the impending change process that will be happening.

It is not unusual for senior managers to be fearful of accepting that they cannot be omnicompetent and authentically delegate responsibility. Where there is evidence of a 'Command and Control' culture and micromanagement is prevalent, then the discussion will concentrate on how the process of the debrief will benefit delegation, team building, and engagement with the subsequent changes.

The process is unique in that all relevant people from the operational, tactical, and executive levels are gathered to share their perspectives, expertise, and insight concerning the subject matter. The Senior Decision Maker and CEO are also present. In this case, the subject matter are the root causes of conflict within the organisation, and suggested remedies.

The presence of the CEO signifies the importance of the event to the organisation. The presence of all relevant attendees has significant resource implications for the organisation. The opportunity cost matters.

The debrief provides a real opportunity for effective team building.

The questions are a combination of role-specific and organisation-wide questions. Therefore, all attendees have an equal opportunity to learn the extent of the knowledge possessed by each other. Nothing is hidden or off-limits.

This wonderful learning opportunity includes both the SDM and the CEO.

They come to realise that not only do they not need to know everything about everything, but it is also evident that they do not know everything. The seeds are being sown for understanding the importance of delegation. The beauty of the debrief lies in the range of information and intelligence gleaned from and by the attendees. This intelligence is highly unlikely ever to have reached the SDM or CEO.

This reality is often called 'The Iceberg of Ignorance '.

The principal cause is fear of professional and personal repercussions by the 'bearer of bad news'! This results in a subtle massaging of the information, so that by the time it reaches the executive level it is almost meaningless.

The extent of the ignorance of the C Suite of the operational reality has been expressed in % terms:

- 4% of problems are known to executives.
- 96% of problems are hidden from senior management.
- 9% of problems are known to team managers.
- 74% of problems are known to team leaders.
- 100% of problems are known to the staff.

The Action Plan that results from the debrief is created entirely from the intelligence that has emerged at the meeting. The resultant action plan is therefore better prepared and more credible than those prepared in the traditional manner.

This helps deliver a higher level of acceptance and engagement by the people in the organisation.

Another added benefit is that the SDM or CEO is more appreciative of the value and potential to delegate because they have seen for themselves the quality of expertise amongst people that they may never have known existed.

The responsibility to deliver these actions can then be based more on expertise and potential for professional development, than on an individual's role in the organisation.

The strategic benefit of the Chrysalis Method of Conflict Resolution for an organisation is that they are provided with clean business intelligence to mitigate or eradicate the objectively identified root causes of conflict.

The value of such benefits can well be imagined.

Case Study

It is relatively easy to think of the cost of conflict in purely financial terms.

For me, the human cost in terms of stress and adverse impact on our business and private lives is almost incalculable.

B was the CEO of a small company employing 30 staff.

They had formed the belief that it was the responsibility of the CEO to be the best at everything, to know everything, and to be responsible for everything.

It was a classic 'Command and Control' culture.

This mistaken belief had been instilled in them by a business coach who was a member of a franchise created in the United States. This 'coach' owed the franchise a lot of costs associated with the privilege of indoctrinating clients to focus just on the bottom line. The intensity of their 'coaching sessions' resulted in the CEO being physically sick with fear and trepidation beforehand!

The CEO approached me for help.

They had devised a new strategy for the development of the business. They were concerned that the staff were dead set against any change and would seek to obstruct its implementation. The intention of the CEO was to close the company if their plans were thwarted by the staff.

The CEO had suffered sleepless nights worrying about how to present the plan to the staff.

None of the staff had been consulted about the strategy in any way at any time.

I explained to the CEO about structured debriefing and asked if I could have a site visit to speak to the staff about their attending a meeting to discuss the development of the company, where their views would be welcomed and respected.

Their response was overwhelmingly positive.

Many of the staff had been employed by the company for years. They were frustrated because, to date, they did not have any involvement in decision-making.

In summary, following the principles I have described above, the debrief was a resounding success.

The CEO realised that the staff cared about the company and could contribute positively to its development. The ideas that the staff outlined in the debrief resulted in both a much-improved strategy and one in which it was evident that they were supportive.

The CEO understood that their belief in being omnicompetent was unrealistic and unnecessary. The staff saw the CEO as a person not simply a role. Communication was improved moving forward, and the CEO delegated responsibility for the implementation of key aspects of the strategy. These were successfully delivered.

The former culture of 'us' and 'them' was replaced by a culture of 'us'. The financial health of the business flourished and, most importantly, the well-being, and mental health of the CEO and staff improved considerably.

Lessons learned included these simple truths:
- The role is not the person.
- We are all people.

The power and benefit of The Chrysalis Method of Conflict Resolution are that it takes a therapeutic approach to traumatised participants to create an environment where people in complex and well-established conflict work together, facilitated by me, to design and create their own sustainable and positive future.

I am honoured that people put their trust and confidence in me to achieve such outcomes for them.

Chapter Twelve

Coda

The following quotes come from General Colin Powell:

'Leadership is solving problems. The day soldiers stop bringing you their problems is the day you have stopped leading them. They have either lost confidence that you can help, or they have concluded that you do not care. Either case is a failure of leadership.'

'Diplomacy is listening to what the other guy needs. Preserving your own position but listening to the other guy. You have to develop relationships with other people so when the tough times come, you can work together.'

'Fit no stereotypes. Don't chase the latest management fads. The situation dictates which approach best accomplishes the team's mission.'

'You don't know what you can get away with until you try.'

'Giving back involves a certain amount of giving up.'

'If a leader doesn't convey passion and intensity then there will be no passion and intensity within the organisation, and they'll start to fall down and get depressed.'

'Don't bother people for help without first trying to solve the problem yourself.'

'I think whether you're having setbacks or not, the role of a leader is always to display a winning attitude.'
    '' In other words, don't expect to always be great. Disappointments, failures, and setbacks are the normal part of the life cycle of a unit or company, and what the leader has to do is constantly be up and say 'We have a problem. Let's go and get it.'

'My own experience is to use the tools that are out there. Use the digital world. But never lose sight of the need to reach out and talk to people who don't share your view. Listen to them and see if you can find a way to compromise.'

'If you are going to achieve excellence in big things, you develop the habit in little matters.

Excellence is not an exception; it is a prevailing attitude.'

'Great leaders are almost always great simplifiers who can cut through argument, debate, and doubt to offer a solution everybody can understand.'

Perhaps my favourite quote is from Ronald Reagan:

'We can't help everyone, but everyone can help someone.'

What do all these quotes have in common? Why have I included these quotes here, and not earlier in my book?

How might these quotes help you to better understand the responsibilities of managing people?

What might you do differently?

What could you do differently?

What is stopping you from making those changes?

Are they reasons or excuses?

Root cause analysis of workplace conflict leaves me with the conviction that effective, proportionate, and appropriate early intervention by managers and supervisors is the key to mitigating the consequences.

Leadership creates the values and culture of the organisation. Thus, managers need to always demonstrate their relevant expertise in their daily behaviours and interactions. It is not a tap that can be turned off or on at a whim if it is to become natural and credible.

Managers and their teams need to know each other as people. The role is not the person. This is a two-way street. We are all people.

Understanding and appreciating that reality is a prerequisite to being able to establish the necessary trust and confidence to be made aware of and initially to have 'difficult conversations.

These conversations can be challenging but are not insurmountable. Goodwill and a positive mental attitude count for a lot when people are fearful of opening up about issues that matter to them.

Equally important is for managers to establish the facts of a situation as far as possible before deciding how best to proceed in the best interests of the people concerned and the organisation.

Remember, people will be watching how you as a manager operate. Fairness, objectivity, neutrality, and impartiality are essential parts of your 'toolkit'.

In my opinion, what people refer to as 'soft skills' should be called 'ESSENTIAL skills'.

Conflict in the workplace is inevitable.

Managers must be able to manage. For them to be as effective as they can be, managers are entitled to be equipped with the necessary skill set to do so. Ideally, senior managers can mentor their development. HR should be a valuable source of professional expertise and advice.

Continuous Professional Development (CPD) should be ingrained in the culture of all people.

What managers have control over is the nature, extent, duration, and impact of that conflict.

The ramifications of relationships breaking down in the workplace are extensive. This extends into our private lives, impacting friends and families.

When a manager has positioned themselves so that they are regarded as even-handed by people in their daily dealings, then those people will have trust and confidence in them. This includes raising issues and responding to reasonable requests for additional information.

The role of HR in organisations should be akin to being an 'a critical friend' to the manager. They are not charged with the management responsibility of the conflicted people. HR should be a trusted resource to ensure that the manager is equipped with the tools and understanding to manage effectively and fairly. HR is not there to replace line management responsibility. The buck stops with the manager.

Unfortunately, in some organisations, roles, and responsibilities can be conflated between HR and managers. In situations where managers lack the understanding of how to manage people, then HR can be mistakenly afforded operational primacy where conflict arises. In effect, HR can drive the process.

Such practices compound the problem of the brand reputation of HR. They are seen to direct investigations and determine outcomes and even sanctions. This is an incorrect use of HR and must be resisted.

The involvement of HR often coincides with the use of formal processes, such as Grievance Procedures or Misconduct.

In the minds of some, workplace mediation, being seen as informal, is not necessarily regarded as 'serious' a process as others. This is an unfortunate misconception since the Written Agreement, uniquely, can deliver a mutually agreeable, 'moral contract' designed by the conflicted participants which describes their future positive and sustainable relationship.

It is truly a win-win.

None of the other forms of conflict resolution can provide this.

I have previously described in more detail how powerful and valuable workplace mediation can be in the context of the dynamics of power. The healing of relationships is a form of Unique Selling Point (USP) compared to other interventions.

The Health and Safety Executive (HSE) in 2007 produced a leaflet 'How to tackle work-related stress'.

HSE STRESS MANAGEMENT STAN

Management Standards (MS) were devised to illustrate to employers and employees the required way in which business is required to be conducted to remain lawful.

I have reproduced the MS for relationships at work as this is pertinent to this book. The following information in quotation marks is from that document.

What is stress and why do we need to tackle it?

'People get confused about the difference between pressure and stress. We all experience pressure regularly – it can motivate us to perform at our best. It is when we experience too much pressure and feel unable to cope that stress can result. The Health and Safety Executive (HSE) estimates the costs to society in the United Kingdom of work-related stress to be around £4 billion each year, while 13.5 million working days were lost to stress in 2007/08. By taking action to reduce the problem, you can help create a more productive, healthy workforce and save money. Many organisations have reported improvements in productivity, retention of staff, and a reduction in sickness absence after tackling work-related stress.

'As an employer, you are also required by law to assess the risk of stress-related ill health arising from work activities and take action to control that risk.'

Management Standard for Relationships

Relationships Include promoting positive working to avoid conflict and dealing with unacceptable behaviour.

The standard is that:
- employees indicate that they are not subjected to unacceptable behaviours, e.g., bullying at work; and,
- systems are in place locally to respond to any individual concerns.

What should be happening/states to be achieved:
- the organisation promotes positive behaviours at work to avoid conflict and ensure fairness.
- employees share information relevant to their work.
- the organisation has agreed to policies and procedures to prevent or resolve unacceptable behaviour.
- systems are in place to enable and encourage managers to deal with unacceptable behaviour.
- systems are in place to enable and encourage employees to report unacceptable behaviour.

"If you identify any issues that cause or aggravate stress at work, employers have a legal responsibility to help their employees. Respond to the issue by involving workers in discussions about possible solutions and action points should be agreed together."

Thus, we can see that promoting good working relationships is not just good business sense but is a legal requirement.

In conclusion, I trust that the need for quality professional development of managers to manage people properly will be recognised as a strategic risk for organisations and businesses.

I can well imagine managers and supervisors thinking to themselves that the picture I paint of the need and value of a human-centric approach is nirvana.

My direct experience of managing and leading teams and departments is that taking the time and effort to know the person, not the role, is the way to go.

Firstly, managers cannot be expected to do the work of their reports themselves.

Secondly, micromanagement is a failed strategy. It wastes time and is bureaucratic, demeaning, and demoralising for people at the receiving end.

Thirdly, authentic team building is a conscious process that is dependent upon 'buy-in' and the engagement of members of the team. It cannot be imposed by diktat or email.

Fourthly, teams are successful based upon their voluntary and discretionary effort in support of an agreed and common cause.

Fifthly, when the situation truly requires the manager to focus the efforts of the team for a specific purpose then the effective relationship built up assists that effort.

Most importantly, having a human-centric approach is good for the well-being of the manager. They become a better person.

Remember, workplace conflict is inevitable, but we have a choice as to how we respond to that challenge.

In the event of workplace conflict arising that cannot be appropriately resolved by a manager, then external, independent, in-person accredited mediation is the best solution for all concerned.

I trust that my book stimulates thinking and debate on the benefits of workplace mediation and the wider aspects of conflict resolution awareness for those people entrusted by organisations to manage people. The impact on people, organisations, and wider society of the consequences of our collective failure to truly learn lessons and reform our systems and processes is profound. The nature and extent of that impact depend upon the choices we make.

www.ingramcontent.com/pod-product-compliance
Lightning Source LLC
Chambersburg PA
CBHW031417210526
45464CB00005B/1920